Introduction to the Webseries:

A Collection of Reviews

Anthony Letizia

Contents

Introduction

It all started with *The Spot*. Created by aspiring filmmaker Scott Zakarin in 1995, this *"Melrose Place* meets *The Real World"* concoction became the Internet's first episodic website. Although it lasted for only two years before folding for financial reasons, it ignited an onslaught of other online webisodics, each hoping to challenge television's supremacy as a storytelling medium.

Such an aim was ahead of its time, however, as Internet video in the late 1990s basically amounted to a two-inch screen of poor quality and low frame rates. It wasn't until broadband developed into a better delivery system and the technology needed to film and edit dropped in price that the lofty ambitions to which *The Spot* had aspired finally became reachable. The Internet landscape is now dotted with a variety of quality webseries, created by independent video makers in locales ranging from Los Angeles to New York, Dallas to Washington and from Pittsburgh to Madison, Wisconsin.

"Quality," of course, is the key word in that sentence. Once video streaming was perfected, a slew of creative wannabes initially hit the World Wide Web. While a few were able to rise above the multitude of "cat videos" on YouTube, most were of a sub par nature with deficiencies that included poor lighting, inconsistent sound quality, mediocre dialogue and bad acting. Fortunately there were enough exceptions to the rule—including Felicia Day's *The Guild*, Matt Sloan and Aaron Yonda's *Chad Vader* and *Something to Be Desired* by Justin Kownacki—to demonstrate the potential of the webseries as a legitimate source of entertainment.

Then came *Dr. Horrible's Sing-Along Blog* and everything changed. Sure, it was created by television producer Joss Whedon and members of his immediate family but it fulfilled the promise of the World Wide Web nonetheless. Whedon, despite his somewhat rebellious nature, was still a Hollywood insider, so it should be no surprise that the three-part Internet musical had a sleek, professional feel. He had amassed enough friends and favors through the years after all, and was even able to land Neil Patrick Harris for the title role. *Dr. Horrible* was still an independent endeavor, however, in that it was crafted outside of the industry norm and showcased what the webseries medium was capable of producing.

Although amateurish webseries still exist, they have been overrun since *Dr. Horrible*'s debut by talented creators with true vision. More significantly, the independent nature of these productions makes them better than most shows currently on television—even if many of them have their roots in the classics of yesteryear. With only a few notable exceptions, most current network sitcoms do not stand up against such standards as *The Dick Van Dyke Show* and *The Mary Tyler Moore Show* or even *Friends* and *Seinfeld*. While retaining their own originality, however, numerous webseries can be considered direct descendents of such comedies—including *The Baristas*, *Copy & Pastry*, *Freckle and Bean* and *Saving Rent*.

The World Wide Web has often been portrayed as the great equalizer in that anyone, regardless of gender, race, orientation or interest, can find an audience. The same holds true for the webseries medium as women—who have often been "outsiders" in the more male-dominated Hollywood—can be considered some of the best and most prolific webseries creators. There's *The Real Girl's Guide to Everything Else*, for instance, which features a Lebanese lesbian as its lead and was created by Carmen Elena Mitchell in order to offer a different female viewpoint of life in the Twenty First Century; *Next! the series* by real life casting director Heather Laird; and *We Are with the Band* by USC graduates Heleya de Barros and Vivian Kerr.

The webseries medium also allows for the exploration of settings that are not usually found on traditional television. Felicia Day originally wrote *The Guild* as a pilot but turned it into a webseries when television insiders considered its focus on a group of online gamers as "too niche." A handful of other webseries, including *Anti-Matter* and *The Variants*, take place in comic book stores. Although one of the early tag lines for the CBS comedy *The Big Bang Theory* declared that "smart is the new sexy," it took the Internet to prove just how true that statement was in a wide variety of ways.

Obviously none of the above observations are meant to suggest that the webseries is poised to overtake television as the predominant source of home entertainment. While there have indeed been a number of successes, the medium has yet to truly hit the mainstream and even fewer have found any sort of financial success. The webseries has, however, produced its fair share of quality entertainment that is on par with—if not better than—the majority of television offerings and that number will hopefully rise in the months and years to come.

In the pages that follow are reviews of just a small handful of the more notable productions that are available for viewing on the Internet. Taken together, these webseries offer the best introduction to not only the medium itself but its promise and potential as well. In the end, I hope you enjoy reading these reviews as much as I enjoyed writing them—and will likewise tune in and experience the world of the webseries for yourself.

Anthony Letizia

The Baristas

In the annals of television sitcoms, the NBC comedy *Cheers* ranks high on the list of all-time classics. With the simple premise of womanizing Sam Malone and uptight intellectual Diane Chambers working side-by-side in the Boston bar that bares the name of the series, *Cheers* provided more that its fair share of laughs as it not only explored the relationship of the two leads but the lives of its exceptional ensemble cast as well. Although the setting for *The Baristas* is a coffee shop instead of a bar, the java-based webseries is more akin to *Cheers* in both style and substance than other NBC sitcoms that have utilized similar locales as the hangout for their characters, including Central Perk on *Friends* and Café Nervosa on *Frasier*.

Like *Cheers*, *The Baristas* begins with an unexpected new addition to the staff of the Affogato coffee shop in which the series takes place. Whereas Diane Chambers is unceremoniously dumped by her fiancé in the pilot episode of the NBC sitcom—leaving her alone and desperate for employment—recently engaged Ben suddenly finds himself unemployed and in need of a job on *The Baristas*. Since Ben's soon-to-be wife's sister is the long-suffering girlfriend of Affogato manager Sam, he is able to join the staff of the establishment and partake in their ongoing humorous interactions with the small but entertaining regular clientele of Affogato.

The Baristas was created by former Pittsburgh resident Justin Kownacki as a spin-off to his successful webseries Something to Be Desired, which premiered online in 2003 and ran for six seasons. Although many of the characters from Something to Be Desired are part of the cast on The Baristas, the newer creation effectively re-introduces them and is enjoyable in its own right in much the same way as Cheers spin-off Frasier. While there are no Sam Malone or Diane Chambers-like leads for the various episodes to focus on, the ensemble cast of the webseries shines nonetheless with its own amalgamation of regulars and co-workers that compliment the narratives just as Carla Tortelli, Woody Boyd, Norm Peterson and Cliff Clavin did on Cheers.

In addition to the struggling-to-keep-the-coffee-shop-afloat Sam (Shaun Starke) and the always optimistic Ben (Will McMahon), the staff at Affogato includes the bitter yet efficient Dierdre (Lacey Fleming), additional newbie Reggie (Aki Jamal), the perpetually chipper Madison (Jillian Vitko) and the likewise upbeat Gary (Joel Ambrose). They are joined in the episodes by such regular customers as Ben's best friend Chase (Justin Mohr), a successful business school graduate with a snobbish attitude; Astrid (Laura Lee Brautigam), an artist who has been dating Sam for six years with no end in sight; Gary's significant other Scott (Hamilton Berube); Ben's controlling fiancé Aubrey (Katie Mo Goff); wannabe writer and decaf-drinking Glenn (Rick Hertzig); Vanity Press publisher Rich (Erik Schark) and his second-in-command Tabitha (Courtney Jenkins); and egocentric author Leo (Will Guffey).

Despite such a large cast, *The Baristas* does an effective job of utilizing the characters throughout the various episodes and allows them to shine in their own unique and humorous ways. The narratives of each installment, meanwhile, feature sitcom-worthy storylines that develop and build as the episode goes along while the scripts are filled with numerous one-liners that keep the comedy rolling. The main plots are likewise complimented with side-bar and secondary scenes that further pack each episode—an amazing feat considering the six-to-seven minute length of the installments.

The third episode of the series, entitled "Game Night," is a prime example. In order to attract new customers and thus potentially increase their work hours, Ben and Madison decide to organize theme nights at Affogato. Their first attempt attracts—as Dierdre phrases it—"three virgins playing *Dungeons & Dragons*." The trio of new females draws the attention of the male regulars of the establishment, however, including publisher Rick who has apparently never played *D&D* before. Sam, meanwhile, steals rolls of toilet paper from various nearby gas stations when the coffee shop restrooms run out of the necessity, leaving girlfriend Astrid to ditch the tow truck that spotted them. The narrative eventually shifts to a discussion of *X-Men* films, a misguided bet and cash stolen from the tip jar.

Like Boston with *Cheers*, or even New York City with *Friends* or Seattle with *Frasier*, *The Baristas* pays homage to its setting of Pittsburgh throughout many of the episodes. Affogato, for instance, is an actual coffee shop in the region and Pittsburgh

City Councilman William Peduto makes a brief appearance at the beginning of "The Competition." In the episode "St. Patrick's Day," meanwhile, references to the Pittsburgh tradition of celebrating the holiday in Market Square are made, as well as remarks regarding other areas within the city limits. "By the time we get to the South Side, all the drunk secretaries are going to be sober enough to want to make small talk again," Chase muses about the notoriously bar-heavy neighborhood.

Justin Kownacki was a pioneer in the online video medium when he launched *Something to Be Desired* in 2003. The long-running webseries attracted a large fanbase as well as critical acclaim and was even a Yahoo! Video Awards nominee for "Best Series" in 2008. With *The Baristas*, he has not only created a worthy spin-off to *Something to Be Desired*, but a genuine comedy classic that is capable of standing on its own merits. *The Baristas* contains all of the ingredients necessary for a quality webseries—well-developed characters, top-notch acting, tight scripts and entertaining narratives. Add the coffee shop setting into the mix, and the sitcom is indeed a *Cheers*-like destination where viewers can ultimately feel glad they visited.

March 28, 2011

Captain Blasto

Like a vast majority of high school students, Christopher Preksta dreamt of being a superhero. "I guess, like a lot of kids, I was thinking that every day seems like the one before and just wishing for something exciting to happen," he explained to the *Pittsburgh Post Gazette* in May 2005. "In high school it was the same—alienated, bored, wondering what it would be like to be a superhero with important things to do."

Fortunately those thoughts never escaped Preksta's mind and he eventually turned the idea into a screenplay called *Captain Blasto*. He quickly discovered, however, that filmmaking could be just as complex as being an actual superhero but persevered nonetheless through the challenges of raising the necessary funds, casting and directing as well as acting, and the arduous task of post-production editing. A road that began in 2002 thus reached fruition in 2005 when *Captain Blasto* premiered at a local Pittsburgh movie theater. While most stories of independent film endeavors end with that one-off screening, Preksta was later able to reinvent his labor of love into an award-winning and successful webseries in 2008.

In many ways, *Captain Blasto* is perfect for the budding new medium. The storyline, for instance, naturally lends itself into being split into eleven short episodes while retaining its overarching narrative. In fact, it's hard to believe that Christopher Preksta did not specifically write *Captain Blasto* as a webseries. And while the creator's use of low-tech equipment—the project was filmed with a Canon XL1 and edited with Adobe Premier Pro—could potentially appear noticeable on a big screen, the final product comes across as professionally polished on a computer monitor.

Quality production values of course mean nothing without a good story and Preksta delivers here as well. Colin (Preksta) is an eighteen-year-old high school student whose best friend is an old 1930s comic book collection centered on the fictitious Captain Blasto. Colin's walls are filled with posters of the character and he even listens to vinyl album recordings of an old radio show broadcast about the superhero.

"In school, nobody pays any attention to me," Colin confides. "Most of them don't even know my name. I walk passed them every day, I sit in class with them, I eat lunch with them and it's like I'm not even there."

He eventually comes up with a solution for his isolated existence by staging fake crimes with the help of high school janitor Daryl (Aaron Kleiber) and then arriving in the nick of time to save the day as Captain Blasto. With Daryl dressed as a silent film era villain—a mask that only covers his eyes and a black and white horizontally striped shirt—the "bad guy" steals toy cars and lemonade from little kids only to be thwarted by Colin's cape-wearing Captain Blasto and a furry of fake punches and kicks.

10

Colin further advances his fantasy by donning Clark Kent-style glasses and applying for a job at the local newspaper, renting an unused warehouse as his lair and outfitting a phone booth with curtains to allow him to readily change into his superhero outfit. Daryl's Hamburglar-esque costume, meanwhile, gets swapped for *Reservoir Dogs*-style white shirt, tie and sunglasses while the crew itself expands with other bored and lonely citizens from the local community.

"We're going to be doing something that's never been done before and it's something fairly dangerous," Colin explains to the group. "And you're all here because you want to do something exciting."

With a larger ensemble, the criminal capers inevitably grow larger as well with fake robberies of small stores. Colin in turn writes about the superhero antics of Captain Blasto for the local newspaper, giving their escapades a level of legitimacy. It turns out to be too much legitimacy, however, when a local police detective starts sniffing around and connects the dots. Still, Colin insists on raising the stakes even further by casting a supervillain.

"Every great hero has their villain," he rationalizes. "Superman has Lex Luther, Batman has the Joker, Green Lantern has the color yellow."

Unfortunately the guy chosen to play the role of Professor Fandango, Evan (Curt Wootton), has plans of his own that conflict with those of Colin. His first appearance, for instance, ends with him walking out because he considers the quilting club targeted as too smalltime for a villain of his stature. A movie theater heist, meanwhile, goes awry when the crowd abruptly exits the building before Captain Blasto can save the day and the gang accidentally leaves with the stolen money. After high school janitor Daryl starts to experience financial problems, the "bad guy" role-playing becomes a little too real and Colin finds himself having to stand up against his self-created band of criminals.

Although this leads to a darker undertone in later episodes, *Captain Blasto* is still a fun and funny romp that brings to mind an older period of storytelling. Christopher Preksta's use of split screens mimics the graphic elements of actual comic books while the chase and fight scenes are reminiscent of Keystone Cops-style slapstick and other black-and-white era Hollywood classics. The musical score, meanwhile, is filled with jazzy riffs that add to the Saturday matinee "serial" quality.

Despite such old-school tendencies and its comic book inspired narrative, *Captain Blasto* also serves as an inspirational tale about the triumph of the human spirit. "We're all so quick to grow up, to become an adult, then we spend the rest of our lives trying to feel the way we did when we were a kid," retired taxi cab driver Sam (Sam Spiegel) tells Colin. "Look at these guys, look at Mike. He was dead. The whole world was walking all over him. Tom? Angry, frustrated. And myself—never had so much fun in my whole life. You've given these guys something they've been looking for their whole lives."

The police eventually catch up with Colin and his crew in the end, but their lives do indeed take a turn for the better nonetheless. Computer technician Mike (Mark Tierno), for instance, loses his job but decides to pursue his childhood dream of becoming an architect in the aftermath. Although Daryl has to put his house up for sale because of financial troubles, meanwhile, he finds a deeper love and appreciation for his kids. Even "supervillain" Evan is transformed by the experience when he decides to abandon his self-destructive alcoholic ways. As for Colin—needless to say he has finally been noticed by his fellow high school classmates.

Captain Blasto may have started out as an independent film produced in Pittsburgh, Pennsylvania, circa 2005 but it found a second life of its own when creator Christopher Preksta re-imagined it as a webseries in 2008. Lead character Colin only wanted to be "noticed" and thanks to the Internet, *Captain Blasto* lives on years later—serving as both a testament to the staying power of the medium and the evolution of the webseries into an alternative narrative device as well.

February 21, 2011

The Confession

Man has debated such concepts as good versus evil, free will versus destiny, perception versus reality and the nature of the human being from the dawn of time. The Greek philosopher Plato utilized the narrative form of "dialogues" to convey the teachings of Socrates, a series of discussions between his mentor and his followers, and numerous authors, playwrights and scriptwriters have followed suite through the centuries to likewise explore the meaning of life and morality. From William Shakespeare's *King Lear* to Samuel Beckett's *Waiting for Godot* to the ABC drama *Lost*, such philosophical inquiries have raged on in various literary forms.

With *The Confession*, the webseries has become the latest narrative medium to tackle many of the concepts raised thousands of years ago in the works of Socrates, Plato and Aristotle. The storyline is simple enough—on Christmas Eve, a professional hitman engages an elderly priest in a series of discussions on the role of faith, the darkness that surrounds the soul, the need for compassion and the evil that perpetrates the world. While the main structure is more fitting for the stage than the screen, with the two characters sitting inside a church confessional, the dialogue is often spliced with scenes from the hitman's life that not only add action into the mix but offer additional insights into the character's persona and beliefs.

The Confession greatly benefits from the two actors cast in the webseries. Kiefer Sutherland portrays the hitman and brings the same intensity and sense of self-righteousness that he embedded into Jack Bauer on the FOX drama *24*. "They possess a lot of the similar skills," Sutherland remarked to *TV Guide* about the two characters before clarifying in regards to his *Confession* persona, "This is a bad guy." Veteran actor John Hurt, meanwhile, is cast in the role of the priest. With a lengthy Shakespearean resume attached to his career, Hurt's performance adds gravitas to the proceedings while likewise raising the narrative to a higher level of dramatic quality.

The Confession begins with Kiefer Sutherland entering the confessional of a church as a lone choir girl sings "Silent Night" in the background. While the character freely admits his sins to John Hurt, he is not looking for redemption or penance but merely understanding. His last victim asked for a moment to "make his peace with God," and the calmness of the man right before Sutherland executes him has rattled the hitman. He thus questions the priest for an explanation on the power of faith, even though he himself dismisses it. From there, the conversation between the two men evolve into the concepts of free will, how there is a darkness in every man and whether certain people deserve to die.

In addition to the philosophical debates, *The Confession* also explores the story of Kiefer Sutherland's character through the use of flashbacks, including his first assignment as a professional killer and the rare moments when he did not follow through on his orders. "It is not for you to decide who lives and who dies," John Hurt tells him in response before psychoanalyzing the character from the aspect of a broken childhood home and the subsequent need for power and attention.

Kiefer Sutherland's hitman likewise explores the character of John Hurt and ascertains that the priest has not always been pure in thought nor in action—in fact, he joined the priesthood in penance for the misguided direction of his own youth. The narrative thus peels away the nature of the two men as the storyline moves along, adding further depth the discussion. Additional tension is provided by the fact that the hitman plans to kill again that evening unless the priest can prevent him, and the ending twist of the final installments not only deliver an effective conclusion to the action but the ever-rising nature of the debate the two had engaged in as well.

Kiefer Sutherland not only stars in *The Confession* but also developed the storyline for the webseries after meeting Chris Young of Digital Broadcasting Group. "Chris started talking about wanting to do a drama, but his criteria was different—a drama in five-minute episodes," the actor told *Entertainment Weekly*. "It was one of those things, like a puzzle over the course of the lunch. It can't be complicated to figure out a story in five minutes, right? I couldn't, and it frustrated the crap out of me. So I went home that night, still thinking about it, and it stayed with me for three days. I was falling asleep when I literally got this idea of a confessional."

The Confession was originally released exclusively on Hulu in late March of 2011. According to GigaOM, the professionally polished webseries began to show a profit within two months, quite a feat even with the star-power of Kiefer Sutherland and John Hurt attached to the project. Digital Broadcast Group has even more revenue avenues to explore in the future, including a full-length DVD and the potential for streaming on Netflix.

The Confession likewise further demonstrates that there is more to online video than short comedy skits or YouTube-style clips of sneezing pandas or toilet-flushing cats. With its philosophically-themed narrative and dialogue-styled structure, *The Confession* is a Twenty First Century descendent of Plato and William Shakespeare—proving that a well-written, well-acted and quality production can find both an audience and success regardless of the medium.

May 30, 2011

Copy & Pastry

Despite a proliferation of original webseries sprouting up on the Internet, it is still somewhat of a rarity to find one produced by truly independent industry outsiders that is also well-written, well-acted, polished and entertaining. *Copy & Pastry*, created by two Berkeley School of Digital Filmmaking graduates, is the epitome of those qualities and demonstrates what can happen when exceptional talent is combined with the entrepreneur nature of the World Wide Web.

The series revolves around two roommates attempting to break into the pastry business and the numerous obstacles and screw-ball comedy situations they find themselves in. Scott McCabe and Tory Stanton, who not only created and wrote the show but star in it as well, have a likeable charm about them and genuine chemistry when they interact. In many ways they were tailor made for each other, a sort of Abbott and Costello, Martin and Lewis and even Laurel and Hardy for the Internet Age.

Copy & Pastry harkens back to those early comedy days in another sense—many scenes are filled with slapstick and the physical comedy abilities of McCabe and Stanton are just as impressive as their writing and acting skills. From McCabe's attempts to pick a blood-donating Stanton up off the floor to the duo making their way to the front of a bookstore lecture, the webseries is filled with such old-school sequences.

Like any quality sitcom, *Copy & Pastry* is also populated with an assortment of oddball supporting characters. There's Patty Plumbopple (Rana Weber), the board of health supervisor whose office is decorated with nude male drawings made by her son; an ill-tempered, foul-mouthed priest who belittles the *Copy & Pastry* caterers for selling baked goods on church property; and Vick (Matt Gunnison), a fake health inspector who gets wasted on marijuana-laced brownies.

The laughs don't stop at the conclusion of each installment, however, as the final sequences feature acappella-style singing and fictional commercials. As the credits roll, McCabe and Stanton are seen in a recording studio performing versions of such songs as the Beach Boys' "Wouldn't It Be Nice," rewritten to reflect the culinary aspect of the series. "Mister Sandman" thus becomes "Mister Tart Man," and "Pour Some Sugar on Me" transforms into "Extra Sugar for Free." Like everything else about *Copy & Pastry*, the vocal performances again prove that McCabe and Stanton are capable of "doing it all" in what often feels like a two-man vaudeville show.

The commercials tacked on at the end, meanwhile, are humorous stand-alones that work just as well. While many remain true to the webseries' theme—such as Pud's Pizza and Mrs. Munchies—others have no connection to the food industry. The end of the third episode, for instance, features a hilarious send-up of Apple's

19

iPhone 3G, called ePhone 3H. "Want to know what your new bride is doing on her lunch break? There's an app for that," the announcer proclaims. "Want to know if the child's yours or not? You better believe there's an app for that."

Although many webseries and independent films often utilize friends and colleagues as actors, McCabe and Stanton went the professional route of seeking talent within the Berkley theater and comedy scene, going so far as to even use a casting director. The two also split the filming of the episodes into phases in order to make their endeavor stronger, funnier and better.

"We wrote and shot episodes one-to-three first, and then cut them together to see which story lines played best," McCabe told *CineSource Magazine* in March 2010. "Then we took a month off to write and pre-produce the last four episodes. This method was validated by the difference in quality, both narratively and technically, of the back half of the season."

Such deviation from the traditional model of filmmaking adds to the appealing quality of *Copy & Pastry*. Although McCabe and Stanton could be considered mavericks to the medium, they still adhered to the basics of webseries creation in regards to the finished product. The writing, for instance, is as tight and funny as anything on television—let alone the Internet—and the under-ten-minute episodes both advance the overall storyline as well as stand on their own merit. The behind-the-camera efforts of director Joel Pincosy and cinematographer Justin Potter, meanwhile, add to the professional tone and quality of the production.

Scott McCabe and Tory Stanton may be new to the world of the webseries medium, but they have proven that they have an innate ability to follow the basics and add new twists to the production process, in the end making *Copy & Pastry* one tasty treat of comedic entertainment.

March 15, 2010

.

Dr. Horrible's Sing-Along Blog

Dr. Horrible's Sing-Along Blog, the much-hyped webseries creation from *Buffy the Vampire Slayer* mastermind Joss Whedon, siblings Jed and Zack, and Jed's fiancé Maurissa Tancharoen, initially hit the Internet during the summer of 2008 and quickly crashed after 200,000 eager viewers-per-hour flooded the website's servers. Simultaneously released on iTunes, *Dr. Horrible* likewise became the top TV download in a relatively short time, and media outlets from *USA Today* to *Variety* dubbed the three-part web "mini-series" a monumental event in the short history of Internet video. The Academy of Television Arts and Sciences honored the series as well, awarding it an Emmy in 2009 for "Short-Format Live-Action, Special Class." Eventually released on DVD (with an accompanying musical commentary), *Dr. Horrible* has even been screened in local theaters, similar to how the musical episode of *Buffy* once stormed across the nation before legal considerations shut it down.

The webseries—which Whedon describes as "the story of a low-rent supervillain, the hero who keeps beating him up, and the cute girl from the laundromat he's too shy to talk to"—stars Neil Patrick Harris as Dr. Horrible, Nathan Fillion (who worked with Whedon on the short-lived FOX drama *Firefly* as well as its big-screen sequel, *Serenity*) as Captain Hammer and Felicia Day (potential slayer Vi in *Buffy*) as Penny. While a musical in style—

and both entertaining and comic in nature—*Dr. Horrible* is actually more detailed and depth-oriented than one might expect; each of the characters evoke a naïve innocence, while the narrative itself explores what happens when that innocence both fades and eventually shatters.

All the elements of *Dr. Horrible* click in top-notch fashion, from the writing to the acting to the music itself. Harris, for instance, shines as the title character. His vocal abilities go beyond impressive to Broadway-quality, while his acting effectively switches from comic to knee-weak-romantic to determined-evil without ever missing a beat. Fillion, meanwhile, portrays the self-indulgent Captain Hammer with straight-forward smugness coupled with the same charisma he brought to *Firefly*'s Captain Malcolm Reynolds. Just as Harris instills a likeable quality in Dr. Horrible despite the character's inherent villainess, Fillion does the same for the arrogant Hammer.

As for Felicia Day, the *Buffy* Season Seven actress similarly strikes the right balance between meek innocence, naïve optimism and a starry-eyed belief in mankind. While her initial vocal performance comes across as a little "weak," this is simply a reflection of Penny, and the singing grows stronger as both the story and the character's confidence evolves. Day brought a full arsenal of both dramatic and comedic acting abilities to her own recent webseries, *The Guild*, and does the same for *Dr. Horrible*, effectively establishing herself as the predominant female talent in the still infant online medium.

The music, although co-written with brother Jed, invokes the same classical vein that Joss Whedon mined in the *Buffy* musical episode, "Once More With Feeling," and runs a full gamut of styles—the initial laundromat sequence is whimsical in nature while later numbers range from rock to a touch of gospel, and the song collection conjures comparisons to both Stephen Sondheim's *Sweeney Todd* and Jonathan Larson's *Rent*. The underlying instrumental score, composed strictly by Jed, effectively evokes the comic-book nature of the webseries while also adding to the impact of the emotional climax.

The inherent comic nature of Joss Whedon is evident throughout the webseries, with some of the funniest moments and dialogue coming in Act III. The resolution of *Dr. Horrible* is also a classic example of his ability to pull the emotional rug out from under the viewer's feet. The inevitable final confrontation between Dr. Horrible and Captain Hammer not only effectively brings the webseries to conclusion, but transforms the two arch rivals from isolated simplicity into full realization of their inherent natures. Suffice it to say that after their epic battle, neither Dr. Horrible nor Captain Hammer will ever be the same again. The whimsical and comic nature of the webseries likewise evaporates in the final musical sequence as the title character completes his evolution from wannabe to full-fledged supervillain, while the simple, abrupt ending adds to the emotional wallop that Whedon has developed into a personal trademark.

In the end, *Dr. Horrible's Sing-Along Blog* is more than a trailblazer on the World Wide Web terrain, but a classic parable about the perils of naïve innocence, "watch what you wish for" lesson-learning and the cost one eventually pays when guided by blind ambition. It is also whimsical, romantic and comedic while equally living up to the "sing-along" wording of its title. The Whedon Clan has created a webseries that not only brings attention to the potential of the online medium, but a forty-two minute narrative masterpiece for these technologically-changing times in which we live.

July 21, 2008

Fourplay in LA

Life can be defined as many things. A journey, a marathon, an adventure. At its most basic, however, life is a series of moments and experiences, snapshots in time stored in our memory banks to remind us of who we are, where we've been and the many friendships we've made along the way. Strung together, they tell a story but they can also be remembered individually, small nuggets that add up to a lifetime. Narratives are the same way—while many have a beginning, middle and end, others can be experienced and enjoyed merely for the individual nature of the moment.

So it is with *Fourplay in LA*, a five-episode webseries about a group of women in their twenties sharing an apartment in Los Angeles. While there is no overarching plot connecting the three-to-six minute installments, they still stand as humorous snippets about life and friendship and being a young female in the Twenty-First Century. And while that may sound simplistic, there is in actuality a modern sophistication surrounding *Fourplay in LA*—the series may not be a West Coast *Sex and the City*, but it has a unique perspective nonetheless that is brought to life by witty, well-written dialogue and enjoyable performances by the quartet of actresses.

The episode titles are straight forward and each installment consists of a series of discussions on a specific topic. "I'm Fat," for instance, starts with Suzie (Erica Rhodes) on a scale which literally reads "fat." While the other characters debate the implication of the revelation, Suzie appears distraught over the lack of compassion from her roommates. "I thought most guys would sleep with anything that moves as long as you're not three-hundred pounds with a mustache and body odor," she pleads at one point.

"I Love You" centers on Annabelle (Amber Nimedez) and the fact that her loser boyfriend said those three little words to her, although technically he didn't. "With him, it's like he's really dedicated to it," she later explains in regards to his constant video game playing. "It's his passion, he's not just procrastinating." "Grapefruit Shake," meanwhile, involves Rhett (Myrah Penaloza) making a concoction that does not include the proper ingredients to be classified as a shake. The true gem of the five episodes, however, is "Vagina," in which Kinsey (Kendrah McKay) returns from a date with a guy who couldn't find her nether region during sex.

"If a guy can't find my vagina on his own, I'm certainly not going to help him," she tells her roommates before adding that he was "poking and prodding in all the wrong places."

"Our series came about one night at Urth Cafe, a tea house in Santa Monica," actress/producer Amber Nimedez explains. "The four of us sitting around, talking about our goals, joking about

27

how it would be funny if we created a webseries about an exaggerated version of our lives. We approached my friend Erica's sister, a writer living across the country in Rhode Island, to write some episodes. She said yes and created five episodes inspired by her interpretation of us through what she read on our Facebook pages."

Hillary Rhodes, the writer friend in question, indeed crafted enjoyable and humorous scripts filled with dialogue that is both crisp and witty despite the limited scope of the subject matter. Some sample quotes include: "Too fat to be thin but too thin to be funny," "We only have one cute outfit for the four of us," and "He's telling me to look hot—do you think he thinks I'm not hot or is he telling me to look hot because usually I'm not?"

In addition to the strong writing, *Fourplay in LA* also has a polished and professional feel to it. A recent MA graduate, Richie Yau, was recruited to film the webseries along with a full roster of stage hands and support staff. Although the episodes could easily have turned into nothing more than a series of talking heads spouting dialogue, the director moves the characters around the sets and gives them natural movements within the situations. This is most evident in the final episode, "Sugarland," in which the four roommates try on various clothes for a Saturday night of LA clubbing—while the action focuses on one character, the others can be seen roaming from room-to-room in the background.

In the end, *Fourplay in LA* takes what could be considered flaws—simplistic plots with no connecting storyline over the course of a limited number of episodes—to craft a series of both amusing and entertaining nuggets about the life of twentysomething females living the California dream. The actresses are endearing, the dialogue natural and realistic and the production value on par with any webseries. And that makes it a winner.

July 5, 2010

Freckle and Bean

Hollywood. The glamour, coupled with the lure of celebrity-status and success, makes it the destination of choice for hundreds of actors and actresses from across the country. In reality, however, Los Angeles is an endless series of meaningless auditions and low-paying service industry jobs that serve as part of a waiting game until that lucky break comes along. Although it seldom does, the trek is still constantly and consistently made by those who believe they can buck the odds. So it is with James and Emma from the webseries *Freckle and Bean*, two actress roommates living their dream even if that dream is always just out of reach.

While the struggles of wannabe actors waiting on tables in the shadows of Los Angeles is a fertile premise for a situation comedy, *Freckle and Bean* actually conjures up memories of Milwaukee rather than Southern California. More specifically, the Shotz Brewing Factory where two twentysomething females likewise attempted to "make their dreams come true" a handful of decades earlier. Although miles apart location-wise, *Freckle and Bean* emulates the spirit of *Laverne & Shirley* nonetheless and is every bit as funny as that 1970s television classic.

Much of the credit goes to Elena Crevello and Heather McCallum, the two real-life friends and struggling actresses who co-created

Freckle and Bean. In their respective roles as James and Emma, they bring a combination of innocence, optimism and enthusiasm to the characters and a chemistry that adds an underlying charm to the webseries. Like Laverne DeFazio and Shirley Feeney before them, there is also an unstated rivalry between these two best friends who look out for each other just the same as they make their way through the undercurrents of modern Los Angeles.

Instead of Lenny and Squiggy living upstairs from them, James and Emma have next door neighbor Ken (Kris Sharma)—another Hollywood wannabe who believes that performing stand-up comedy routines at an old age home is a prime career path. James and Emma also rent out their dining room area as a "third bedroom" to the silent but always lurking Chase (Bobby Gold). Then there's Skye Holloway (Betsy Cox), a Paris Hilton-like celebrity that James has somehow befriended and continually runs to the aid of when the paparazzi has her cornered. The snobbish Joie (Bailey Conway) and James' boyfriend Oliver (Joshua Snyder) round out the cast.

While the situations that James and Emma find themselves in may be different than those of Laverne and Shirley, they are just as entertaining and funny. From watching Ken perform stand-up comedy at the Bel Air Home for Senior Citizens ("Why do they call them coffins anyway, you're not doing any coughing in there"), to James purchasing an eight-ball in a darkened alley for Skye while dressed in urban attire ("Yo, no, check it, word"), to Emma securing a date with a major actor and his dog ("This guy is a freak"), to James throwing a quarter at another girl talking to

Oliver ("I hit her in the head with a quarter, she could have died"), *Freckle and Bean* is filled with small scenes of high comedic proportion that ultimately tie together to form an exceptional webseries.

"The show is essentially based on our lives in Los Angeles, but we wanted to make it a little more off-beat and quirky, and create a really colorful world that the characters, Freckle and Bean, inhabit," webseries co-creator Elena Crevello explains. "But every story pretty much comes from our own experiences with celebrities in Los Angeles, auditions, boyfriends, friends, etc. Some of the lines in the show are even just direct quotes from either ourselves or things people have said that we have found ridiculous and just put in the show."

Crevello and Heather McCallum actually created *Freckle and Bean* during the Writers Guild of America strike of 2007 and 2008. With the uncertainty of work opportunities looming overhead, the two actresses decided to take fate into their own hands and produce their own showcase. "We were feeling frustrated as actors with what auditions were being offered to us and wanted to create a show that we would enjoy and characters we would want to play," Crevello says. But even after the writing was completed, they discovered the pitfalls and obstacles involved in such an endeavor.

"We shot this show actually two years ago," Crevello elaborates, "but had so many issues with getting it edited, and some former editor of ours deleted a bunch of footage which set us back, and then also getting a website up, funding, etc., that it took us forever to launch the show."

But launch it they did, a feat that is a true testament to their determination and belief in their creation. Which is fortunate, as *Freckle and Bean* is an entertaining webseries and enjoyable addition to the growing medium. Emma may have "freckles" and James may be tall and thin like a "bean," but their comedic antics are a welcome throwback to the "golden age of television sitcoms" and one of its most underrated entries, *Laverne & Shirley*. The two female roommates of *Freckle and Bean* share the same hopes and dreams as the two Shotz Brewery workers, albeit in a different time and setting, and their quest to achieve those dreams resonate today just as much as the did in the past.

In fact, one can almost imagine James and Emma, as well as their real-life counterparts Elena Crevello and Heather McCallum, linking their arms together while shouting, "Schlemiel! Schlimazel! Hasenpfeffer Incorporated!"

December 15, 2010

Fresh Hell

Celebrities have a long history of doing stupid things. From the legal problems of Paris Hilton and Lindsay Lohan, to answering machine rants by Alec Baldwin and Mel Gibson, to Tom Cruise bouncing up-and-down on a couch on *Oprah*, to Charlie Sheen declaring he has "tiger's blood," both the tabloids and mainstream media are filled with stories of high-profile meltdowns. Some of these celebrities have been able to rebuild their careers afterwards, and some never will.

Then there's Brent Spiner, the actor who portrayed the android Data on *Star Trek: The Next Generation*. Both the man and the character are amongst the most popular from the *Star Trek* universe, and Spiner continues to attend conventions in order to interact with the fandom. By all indications, he is a class act with great range as a thespian and an inherent sense of humor. All three of those characteristics shine through in the comedy webseries *Fresh Hell*, in which Spiner mockingly portrays himself as a fallen celebrity living a lonely and isolated life in a small apartment after his own high-profile meltdown, simply referred to as "the incident."

"Where you lost everything," a talk-show host comments about the event. "Your family, your home. Your wealth, your career. Your adoring fans."

Fresh Hell never reveals what it is that Brent Spiner did to make him a toxic outcast, but the first episode of the webseries portrays "the incident" as an extreme example of celebrity misbehavior. "I can imagine a scenario where OJ (Simpson) redeems himself," a guest on the same talk show later remarks. "I mean, it's not like he's Brent Spiner." The host simply replies, "We had a guest on yesterday whose face was literally ripped off by a pit bull. You know what she said to me? 'At least I'm not Brent Spiner.'"

While the specifics of "the incident" are left for the imagination of the viewer, Spiner's quest for rehabilitation falls on the shoulders of next door neighbor and wannabe porn star Dakota (Kat Steel). Through the course of *Fresh Hell*, she convinces the once-famous persona to be her partner at an acting showcase—with a "lost episode of *Friends*" as their script—as well as introduces him to her boyfriend-slash-agent and the psychic-slash-personal manager who lives upstairs in their apartment building. The encounters only add to the level of hell that Brent Spiner finds himself in as the trio of characters are both sitcom-style quirky and funny in their own right.

Agent Tommy (Brian Palermo), for instance, tells Spiner that he can arrange meetings between the former Data and writer/directors J.J. Abrams and Joss Whedon but needs to see his penis first. "I'm putting something out there—my time, my energy, the great name of this firm—and I think you should put something out there, too," Tommy explains before discussing how he helped British actress Judi Dench with her own career.

"She sat in that chair right there, slowly crossed and uncrossed her legs and BOOM! that very day I had her in a film with Vin Diesel."

Psychic Valerie (Karen Austin), meanwhile, later pleads with Spiner to hire her. "I'm the perfect manager for you," she says. "I'm borderline delusional. Have been for years. I follow my instincts no matter how much hard evidence I come up against. And I will put those skills to work for you. I will believe in you delusionally and as your manager, I will infect other people with that delusion."

Brent Spiner co-created *Fresh Hell* with Christopher Ellis and Harry Hannigan. While Spiner is obviously the star of the webseries, Ellis directs the episodes with a high-quality flair while Hannigan delivers scripts filled with crisp dialogue and funny one-liners. When Tommy shows his own irregularly-shaped penis, for example, Spiner remarks, "That thing looks like Owen Wilson's nose."

The acting in *Fresh Hell* is also top-notch, from Kat Steel's infectious portrayal of the bubbly air-head Dakota, to Brain Palermo's serious demeanor and dead-pan delivery as Tommy, to Karen Austin's ability of bringing out the quirky nature of Valerie. Still, the webseries belongs to Brent Spiner and he delivers a comic performance that does not disappoint—everything from his facial expressions to his body language to his recital of the dialogue is spot-on as he maneuvers his way through the personal hell that he suddenly found himself trapped within.

Fresh Hell is fiction of course, as there was no actual "incident" in Brent Spiner's life. Give the man credit, however, for allowing himself to be mocked in such an out-of-character fashion. And thank him as well, along with Christopher Ellis and Harry Hannigan, for creating a comic webseries that is funnier than a majority of the sitcoms that have found their way onto network television in recent years.

Because in the end, *Fresh Hell* is a heavenly form of "fresh entertainment."

June 6, 2011

The Guild

Cyd Sherman's life is complicated. "It's Friday night and still jobless," she tells her webvlog. "Haven't left the house in a week. My therapist broke up with me." She then pauses for a moment before adding with a shrug, "Oh, yeah, there's a gnome warlock in my living room, sleeping on my couch." With that simple introduction begins the first episode of the online webseries *The Guild*. Created and written by actress Felicia Day—who also plays the aforementioned Cyd, aka Codex—this award-winning series follows a group of *World-of-Warcraft*-style online gamers who suddenly find themselves forced to face real-world obstacles when Codex's life takes a screwball-comedy turn for the worse.

Day, who admits to having had a two-year addiction to *World of Warcraft*, originally wrote the script as a television pilot but when she was told that the plot was too "niche," turned it into a webseries instead with the assistance of fellow producers Jane Selle Morgan and Kim Evey. "I decided to write something to show the world that gamers weren't just guys in their twenties who lived in their mom's basement," she told *WoW Insider* in August 2007. "That cliché has become so annoying. I love doing comedy and I wanted to write something that didn't make fun of gamers but was funny to gamers and non-gamers alike."

Felicia Day has indeed populated *The Guild* with an assortment of non-stereotype characters, ranging in age from their late-teens to middle-age, and each carrying their own neurotic behaviors and tendencies. Vork/Herman Holden (Jeff Lewis), for instance, is the eldest of the group and brings his own cheese slices to restaurants in order to not pay the price difference between a hamburger and a cheeseburger. ("I want to grow my money," he says, "not spend it on cheese-gouging.") Tinkerballa (Amy Okuda) appears to be in her early twenties and resists revealing any personal information about herself to the rest of the group, insisting that her real name is the same as her avatar and using the plot of Ugly Betty to explain how she earns a living. ("I like you guys the way you are," she responds when Codex first raises meeting face-to-face. "Cartoon characters who let me feel a sense of achievement in an imaginary world.") Clara (Robin Thorsen), meanwhile, really does use her given name as her online moniker. A mother of three, she is forgetful, a little bit clueless and often neglects her children in favor of gaming. ("My husband's in pharmaceuticals," she tells the group, "and I stay at home with the kids where I'm in pharmaceuticals, too.")

Zaboo/Sujan Balakrishnan Goldberg (Sandeep Parikh) is a college student who eventually serves as the catalyst for Codex's life to spiral downward—mistaking his fellow female cohort's online interaction for that of affection, he arrives at her doorstep with suitcase and laptop in hand, ready to "woo." Bladezz/Simon (Vincent Caso), the youngest of the group, adds to the mayhem when he's banned from the game for twenty-four hours, posts an inappropriate video depicting the Guild's cartoon avatars naked and refuses to return the group's "bank" that he has been entrusted to guard.

Despite all the chaos around her, Codex eventually learns to cope not just with the events of the first season but her isolated and neurotic life as well. It turns out that her father was actually gay; the same for a former boyfriend, a musician who's cello Codex apparently set on fire. Codex, meanwhile, is a violinist. "You know, former child prodigy," she explains. "Now I'm old." In the initial episode, her therapist tells her, "You can't grow if you're still immersed in an imaginary social environment." Codex, in one of her webvlog entries, even reveals that "I just don't cope well. With anything. I mean, there's always a lot of drama in the game, but at the end of the night you can always just log off. You can't log off from your life." But as the comedic escapades of Zaboo and Bladezz escalate, Codex finds an inner strength that gives her the needed confidence to rally the online group of gamers to real world action. "We can do this, OK? With just a few of us we can take down a ten-man dungeon. Life can't be that much harder."

Give Felicia Day her due—she has crafted a solid, layered plot with three-dimensional characters and witty-yet-intelligent dialogue in a medium that consists of three-to-eight minute episodes; many traditional television sitcoms fail to achieve the same blend despite numerous years of production. And although all the actors bring the right balance of comedy and emotion to their roles, it is Day who truly shines as the psychologically damaged Codex, demonstrating exceptional comic-timing with her vocal tones, body language and facial expressions.

The efforts of cast and crew alike were duly rewarded as *The Guild* has already won numerous awards, including the 2007 YouTube Award and 2008 Yahoo! Video Award for "Best Series," as well as the 2008 South by Southwest Greenlight Award for "Best Original Digital Season Production." The first season, meanwhile, amassed over nine million hits. As further testament to the show's quality, a majority of the episodes were financed by fan donations, proving that *The Guild* is both a critical and popular success.

The webseries medium may still be relatively new, but with well-rounded creative talents like Felicia Day amongst the fray, it can expect to have a long and prosperous life.

May 26, 2008

The Last Man(s) on Earth Webseries Review

In the hands of Hollywood, the end of the world has arrived numerous times and in an equal number of ways. On the big screen, for instance, there have been meteors (*Armageddon*) and comets (*Deep Impact*) that have pounded the Earth, viruses that eradicated mankind (*Twenty-Eight Days Later* and *Twelve Monkeys*) and natural disasters—including earthquakes (*Earthquake*), volcanoes (*Volcano*) and tsunamis (*The Perfect Storm*)—that have laid waste to vast regions. The small screen, meanwhile, has witnessed nuclear attacks (*Jericho*), alien invasions (*Falling Skies*) and even zombies (*The Walking Dead*).

With the firm conviction that any one of these events could indeed happen, producer Joe England, director Eric Dove and actors Brady Bloom and Charan Prabhakar have created a series of online videos outlining how to survive such disasters. Taken together, the subsequent webseries *The Last Man(s) on Earth* serves as both a quick primer as well as humorous take on society's obsession with world-ending tragedies.

For the two main characters in *The Last Man(s) on Earth*—Kaduche (Prabhakar) and Wynn (Bloom)—the end of the world is slated to occur in 2012. While they do not know the exact means of Earth's extinction, they are nonetheless prepared for any potential possibility. "We're experts," Wynn explains in the first episode. "We've seen every disaster film at least twice." Each subsequent installment features Kaduche and Wynn explaining survival tips with both flair and conviction, but the scenes of the two characters dressed as commandos are fantasy rather than reality as they also appear more casually attired while having far less luck completing the task at hand.

In "Accumulating Weapons," for instance, the duo are initially seen showcasing such items as bowling pins, weed whackers and rakes. "I feel like I'm planting a garden, not surviving the end of the world," Kaduche frustratingly tells Wynn. "None of this stuff is dangerous." He then offers his own version of the episode, and the characters transform from two average-looking individuals sitting on their front porch into bad-ass Rambos with guns, swords, butcher knives and wooden stakes. "You're friends may turn against you," Kaduche states in a voice-over as he is chased by a zombie Wynn. "Weapons never do."

According to Brady Bloom and Charan Prabhakar, the idea for *The Last Man(s) on Earth* was the melding of two separate sources of inspiration. The first was from director Eric Dove, who witnessed a twister in the California desert. "He wanted to make a webseries about two guys that chase dust twisters, and every episode would be that they didn't find a dust twister because they're just completely unreliable," Bloom explained to *Bricks of the Dead* in July 2011. Later, producer Joe England stumbled upon the concept that the end of the world would arrive in 2012. "We mashed that together with the lameness of the two guys chasing dust twisters and with how the end of the world would be," Bloom continued. "And that kind of brought together that these guys are really lame guys, but they think they're really cool."

The coupling of the "lame" with the "cool" can be seen in both the fantasy and reality scenes of *The Last Man(s) on Earth*. In the fifth episode of the webseries, for instance, Kaduche shoots Wynn in order to demonstrate how to survive a gunshot wound. In the "cool" mind of his onscreen persona, Kaduche places Wynn in a bathtub, sedates him with pain killers, places a sock in Wynn's mouth to mute his screams and removes the bullet with a pair of scissors. In the installment "Fire," meanwhile, real life Kaduche becomes frustrated when Wynn forgets to douse a pile of wood with gasoline before his partner drops a lit match on it. The frustration grows when it turns out to have been the last match and Kaduche becomes pressed for time. "I need to be home by six," he tells Wynn.

Kaduche eventually attempts to start the fire by rubbing two sticks together, but this proves futile as well. "Even in my fantasy this is impossible," his alter-ego laments.

The "episode within an episode" structure suits *The Last Man(s) on Earth* well. While the actual survival video scenes are entertaining and enjoyable in their own right, the "making of" element adds cohesiveness to the series while bringing the characters of Kaduche and Wynn more fully to life. Actors Brady Bloom and Charan Prabhakar, meanwhile, handle the dual "lame" and "cool" aspect of their onscreen personas with pinpoint precision, and director Eric Dove balances reality and fantasy equally effectively, with an overexposed tint to the "fantasy" scenes. The special effects—which include zombie decapitations and exploding vehicles and buildings—complete the cinematographic aspects of the production, while the scripts by writer Aaron Hultgren sustain and balance the action with the comedy, not just within each episode of *The Last Man(s) on Earth* but over the duration of the webseries as a whole.

The destruction of mankind for which Kaduche and Wynn are preparing may or may not occur in 2012, but *The Last Man(s) on Earth* is an excellent way to pass the time until the end of the world actually arrives nonetheless.

July 20, 2011

Next! the series

"There's a lot of glamour in the film industry," professional casting director John Jackson explains at the beginning of the NAPTE LA TV Festival Award Winning webseries, *Next! the series*. "And a lot of work, a lot of hard work. Directors, actors, writers—they're all very, very important. Somebody has to find that talent and that's where I come in." Jackson should obviously know as he has cast a number of films, including *Election*, *About Schmidt* and *Sideways*, throughout his exemplary career. Although he portrays himself in *Next!*, however, the webseries is not an actual documentary of his work but a fabricated interpretation that melds fact with fiction into a fun-filled romp and behind the scenes peak at the casting director profession.

Next! is filmed as a mock reality show following Jackson as he conducts a series of auditions for roles in a low-budget horror film called *The Blamed*. What starts off simple enough snowballs into a hilarious nightmare as the producer and director of the flick not only insist on sitting in on all of the auditions but make casting demands that border on both sexism and racism. The role of a murdered stripper, for instance, needs the sense of realism that can only be achieved—in their eyes, at least—by the part being portrayed by an actual stripper. With a newly installed pole in the middle of the casting room, the auditions begin but eventually turn into a series of lap dances for the producer and

46

requests to see the girls naked. Jackson, the ever consummate professional, obviously puts the kibosh on that idea.

Later, the group conducts auditions for the role of a bus driver who is hijacked by a man with a gun. The producer and director insist on the part going to an African American but the experienced actors who attend the casting call fail to live up to their white, middle-class perception of how black people speak in America.

In addition to the actual auditions for *The Blamed*, the webseries contains a subplot revolving around a faux reality series about sexually active seniors entitled *Golden Swingers*. In order to reach as many potential participants as possible, assistant casting director Kasi Brown posts a casting call on Craigslist in addition to the normal trade publications but inadvertently lists the title of the show as "Golden Showers."

"It's not a porn show," Brown later explains to the camera. "It's very sweet and about seniors finding love and passion."

While the premise of *Next!* is solid enough to warrant the attention of webseries aficionados, the series also benefits from a well rounded cast of characters who add additional wit and charm to the narrative. John Jackson, for instance, gives a strong, nuanced performance as he attempts to balance the impressive resume he has crafted through the years with getting stuck casting a low budget horror flick for a group of low class producers. The professional in him attempts to keep the process focused and on track but his expressions and body language give away the obvious frustration of the task at hand.

Kasi Brown, meanwhile, shines as Jackson's assistant—who is likewise named Kasi Brown. *Next!* again blurs the line of fact and fiction by using the actual resume of the real Brown, an actress who has appeared in such shows as *ER* and *Monk*, for the fictitious Brown. In the webseries, Kasi Brown has no actual ambition in the casting end of the business but is merely using it as a stepping stone to building an acting career.

"She frequently gets in her own way," Jackson comments in regards to Brown and acting. "She sabotages herself and worse of all, she wants to read for every single role whether she is appropriate for it or not. I said you're not a seventeen year old, five-foot nine Italian model who grew up in the Bronx. You're not. This is not the theater. You know, we can't float some menopausal ex-gymnast by wires and pass her off as Peter Pan."

Next! is the brainchild of Kansas City area casting director Heather Laird and the basis for the webseries came from her own personal experiences within the industry. "I have at least four stories in my casting experience where some director wanted strippers, exotic dancers, tassel dancers," she told the *Kansas City Examiner* in July 2010. In addition to developing the concept of *Next!*, Laird also co-wrote the scripts and served as the series' director.

Next! was entered into the 2010 NAPTE LA TV Festival—an independent television festival that likewise spotlights the webseries medium—where it took home the award for Best Comedy Webisode. With its reality show style, behind the scenes look at the casting profession and blending of fact with fiction, *Next!* is not only worthy of the honor but a witty and wonderful webseries creation that is guaranteed to entertain viewers without reaching for the mouse and clicking "next" themselves.

October 8, 2010

Odd Jobs

Although the economic crisis that began in 2008 has wreaked havoc on an untold number of households, the aftereffects have woven their way into numerous comedic outlets nonetheless. The NBC sitcom *The Office*, for instance, has contained narratives centered on layoffs, consolidation, plummeting stock prices and corporate takeovers. The FX comedy *It's Always Sunny in Philadelphia*, meanwhile, spoofed the mortgage crisis and government bailouts in the episodes "The Gang Exploits the Mortgage Crisis" and "The Great Recession." But it is not just television that has developed such storylines in these dark and dire days as a number of webseries have also used the economy as a catalyst for original and insightful comedic endeavors.

In *Saving Rent*, advertising manager Mike loses his job and resorts to renting out rooms in his large house to a group of strangers. *Candy Girls* likewise uses the tough job market for its premise of an MBA graduate launching an escort service when he is unable to find employment in his field. And then there's *Odd Jobs*, an award winning webseries that follows investment banker Nate Brooks (Jeremy Redleaf) when he loses his $90,000 a year corporate job and is forced to find an alternative means to make ends meet.

Like Mike in *Saving Rent* and Jason in *Candy Girls*, Nate attempts to keep his employment status a secret from his girlfriend/fiancé Cassie Stetner (Alexandra Daddario). It is a difficult task, however, as the high maintenance Cassie is accustomed to dining in only the finest restaurants and thinks nothing of spending $15,000 on a wedding dress. Thus enters Nate's slacker roommate Joe Bannon (Devin Ratray), who offers that the best way to make a living in tough economic times—or in any times, for that matter, if one wants to put forth the least amount of effort—is through a series of "odd jobs" that can easily be found on Craigslist in cities across the country. Before you know it, Nate is making $300 as a background dancer in a rap video, pawning candy bars as a fundraiser for a fictitious kids' baseball team and serving as a wine expert at a blind taste-testing session.

Odd Jobs was named "Best New Webseries" at the 2010 Streamy Awards and also received recognition from the NAPTE LA TV Festival and the New York Television Festival. Upon viewing the webseries, it is easy to understand why such accolades were laid at the feet of *Odd Jobs* as just about everything regarding the production works to perfection. First, there are the actors, who bring a natural and likeable quality to their performances. Next, there's the writing, which is filled with wit and originality. And lastly, there's the various "situations" of this situation comedy, which translates into many memorable comedic moments.

Take the opening scene of the first episode in which Nate loses his job. Instead of being just another example of corporate downsizing to cut costs, the catalyst for Nate's inevitable unemployment status is a Broadway musical adaptation of the late 1970s/early 1980s television sitcom *Diff'rent Strokes* that closed on opening night. "Could have been an urban *Annie*," the CEO of the company where Nate works explains during a conference room meeting. "But unfortunately, gentlemen, it flopped. That's on us, we're lead investors." He then resorts to "eenie meenie miney mo" in order to decide who amongst the staff will lose their jobs because of the debacle.

As Nate Brooks, Jeremy Redleaf—who also wrote and created *Odd Jobs*—brings a wide-eyed neurotic innocence to the character and various predicaments he finds himself in during his search for gainful employment. That innocence suits Nate well as he initially struggles with the various "odd jobs" he takes on, only to then find success by the end of the assignments. "I can't dance, it's taken me twenty-five years to learn the electric slide," he explains during a rap video audition but then becomes the featured performer in "Do the Chump" (as the song is called) precisely because of his lack of rhythm. While he is nervous and uncertain making a candy bar sales pitch on a New York subway, the crowd buys the product in droves nonetheless. And although Nate knows nothing about wine, his nonsensical interpretations during the blind taste test comes across as refreshing, earning the title of "hometown retro."

The slobbish Joe Bannon is likewise played to perfection by Devin Ratray, best known as big brother Buzz McCallister in the *Home Alone* films. While the character could easily come across as a slimy huckster, Ratray brings a likeableness to Joe that makes him more loveable than repulsive despite being a borderline slacker con-artist. Joe Bannon is also blessed with some of the best dialogue in *Odd Jobs*, which is saying a lot considering the witty and well-written nature of the scripts. This even extends beyond the closing credits of the fourth episode, in which Joe sits in front of a computer monitor wearing a graduation cap and gown while celebrating the completion of an online college program with his fellow students.

"I believe the leaders of tomorrow are Skype-ing here today," he announces to the webcamera. "Someone in one of these very chat windows may one day design the logo of a company that goes on to cure cancer. It takes an e-village to raise an e-grad, and this guy couldn't have done it without each and e-every one of you. We took the hyperlink less clicked upon and that has made all the difference. Anything is possible when you put your mouse to it. When we look back on the past twenty-two weeks, we're going to say these were the best web hours of our lives."

Odd Jobs is a very funny and original webseries that explores the various options available to anyone looking to earn some quick cash in a very unique fashion. The main website for *Odd Jobs* not only contains the episodes of the show but a slew of information and advice on how to become an odd jobber in the real world as well. Called *Odd Job Nation*, visitors are likewise able to join the discussion and post actual jobs that are found on Craigslists across the country.

Jeremy Redleaf has thus not only crafted an entertaining webseries but created an entire contingent of odd job followers in the process. Now that's impressive.

November 29, 2010

Out of Luck

If you will excuse the pun, leprechauns have been getting the short end of the stick in recent years. While *True Blood* has helped transform vampires into brooding sexual creatures of the night, leprechauns remain the ever-smiling spokesmen for kids' cereal. While the AMC drama *The Walking Dead* have made zombies cool again, the impish mystical beings from Ireland have mostly been forgotten. Even Buffy Summers, who has faced off against every supernatural being known-and-unknown to man, brushes their influence and even existence aside. "There are two things I don't believe in," she states on the former WB/UPN series *Buffy the Vampire Slayer*. "Coincidence and leprechauns."

The lack of attention and respect that leprechauns have been subjected to in contemporary pop culture has come to an end, however, with the advent of the webseries *Out of Luck*. In it, the Irish folklore of old is re-imagined in the form of Patrick (Patrick Newman), a traditionally green-clad leprechaun with a never-ceasing smile and the ability to grant three wishes to whoever catches him. Patrick is as mischievous as any leprechaun of myth, and possesses a "horny" side to go along with the customary attributes of his kind. When likeable loser Jake (Eric Wood), for instance, first stumbles upon him, Patrick is hiding in the trees with a pair of binoculars trained upon the window of Jake's friend Alex (Amanda Rose). Later, Patrick promises to bring an attractive blonde woman back to Leprechaun City and show her his pot of gold.

"That's a euphuism," he explains in case anyone fails to understand his true intentions.

Jake inevitably "catches" Patrick when he falls from the tree in front of Alex's apartment and is granted three wishes for his effort. Just as Major Anthony Nelson received more than he bargained on *I Dream of Jeannie*, however, Jake's world is turned upside down with the introduction of a leprechaun into his life. When Jake uses one of his three wishes to have Patrick "take care" of his overdue rent, the mischievous Irish imp employs a baseball beat to intimidate the landlord as opposed to borrowing funds from his pot of gold. When Jake later gives his third wish to Patrick, matters grow worse as a leprechaun is not allowed to grant their own desires. Patrick thus loses his powers but makes a new deal with Jake in the aftermath—if Jake assists with his dilemma, the leprechaun will help Jake turn his platonic friendship with Alex into a romantic one.

While the idea of a smallish Irishman eternally dressed as if it was St. Patrick's Day seemed like an outlandish concept to Buffy Summers, in the hands of writer/director Riley Workman it comes across as a comic hybrid of fish-out-of-water and reluctant buddy narratives. Much of the appeal of *Out of Luck* has to do with Patrick Newman, who gives the leprechaun an element of natural and genuine charm, but in reality all of the actors in the webseries give top-notch performances. Although the main plot may have the same roots as many traditional and classic sitcoms, the storyline has an original feel to it nonetheless and keeps the audience both laughing and entertained throughout its episodes.

The rise of the webseries medium as legitimate creative outlet has enabled independent productions to tap into the inherent talent-pool of any city anywhere in the country. Just like *The Baristas*, *The Bitter End* and *Chad Vader* were able to utilize residents of Pittsburgh, Montreal and Madison, Wisconsin, in their webseries efforts, *Out of Luck* likewise relies on the local community for both cast and crew. "Our actors are all across the board in terms of experience, but everyone is based in Utah," actor Patrick Newman remarks. "We have our own composer who recently graduated from BYU as well so all of the music is created in-house, even our theme song." Newman himself is a theater student at Brigham Young University while writer/director Riley Workman studies film at nearby Utah Valley University.

According to Newman, it was Workman who developed the idea for *Out of Luck* and approached him to portray the leprechaun. "Riley loves stories that mix mythology with reality and so he dreamt this really fun world up," he explains. "There have been some creative compromises along the way as we have had problems with casting and such, but ultimately Riley wanted to have a fun universe with enjoyable characters that are both in and way out of reality."

In many ways a leprechaun is indeed as "way out of reality" as one can get but *Out of Luck* transports the mystical Irish incarnation of old into a modern-day world inhabited by realistic characters and the dramas of everyday life. Like any good sitcom, it combines the "situation" of the narrative with the "comedy" in an effective and effortless manner while adding quality performances and production values to top it all off. None of that would mean anything, of course, if the narrative itself didn't shine—and for *Out of Luck* it shines like a pot of gold.

Just don't tell Buffy Summers.

June 27, 2011

The Power Object

I have to admit that when I first read the basic premise of the webseries *The Power Object*, I was a bit skeptical. As described by creator Claire-Dee Lim, the show "follows the adventures of three young San Francisco women who turn their loser lives around with the help of a magic vibrator." Adding to my cynical view was the fact that *The Power Object* used dolls as actors as opposed to actual human beings. "Think *Team America* meets *Sex and the City*," Lim offers, referring to the 2004 motion picture from *South Park* gurus Trey Parker and Matt Stone and the classic HBO series starring Sarah Jessica Parker.

Despite my misgivings, I decided to watch the first episode of *The Power Object* with the expectation that I would switch to a different website within sixty-seconds of viewing. In reality, however, I could not have been more wrong as both the overall narrative and inherent humor of the webseries quickly became apparent. While *Team America*, as well as the Seth Green co-created *Robot Chicken* on Adult Swim, utilizes marionettes and action figures for satirical observations on culture and society, *The Power Object* is indeed more akin to the realistically-grounded *Sex and the City*. The story of three college roommates who had big dreams for the future only to find disappointment afterwards is universal after all, and while the use of a "magic vibrator" may be off-beat—to say the least—*The Power Object* likewise contains a cautionary tale of "watch what you wish for" storytelling.

The Power Object centers on Glenda, Hannah and Jessie, whose lives did not turn out the way they expected. Glenda, for instance, had plans of becoming an investigative journalist but finds herself thirty-years-old and working as a researcher for a local television morning show. Jessie, meanwhile, wanted to be a record producer but instead ended up as a "baby-sitter to the stars" as she watches over the musicians signed to the company where she is employed. And Hannah is a sculptress who was unable to find traditional success and now crafts items more suitable for the bedroom than an art gallery.

"I thought my life would be so much different," she laments. "I'd be an artist and married and surrounded by babies. Instead I'm making fake penises all day."

With their lives finding little satisfaction from either a career or romantic standpoint, the three roommates drown their sorrows in bottles of wine before they discover an old spell-book one night and decide to take desperate measures. Like the Halliwell sisters from the former WB series *Charmed*, Glenda, Hannah and Jessie utilize their own "Power of the Three" to make their working-lives more successful. When the next day yields results, the trio turn to a more potent spell and create a literal "power object" that is capable of turning their wishes into reality. The "object" in question, of course, turns out to be a vibrator.

"This is insane," Glenda remarks afterwards. "I'm Phi Beta Kappa, have an IQ of 154. I can't entrust my future to a plastic, battery-operated penis. Can I?"

According to creator Claire-Dee Lim—who co-wrote the family-themed motion picture *Firehouse Dog*—the inspiration for producing a webseries originated during the 2007 strike by the Writers Guild of America. For content, she turned to an old screenplay likewise entitled *The Power Object* that was based on a story crafted with her *Firehouse Dog* partners Mike Werb and Michael Colleary. "A few years ago I was really into *Sex and the City* and *Buffy the Vampire Slayer*, so I wanted to mix the idea of female friendship with a supernatural comedy element," Lim told *Animation Magazine* in June 2011 about the script. "I'm also a huge fan of wish fulfillment stories. Having one's dreams come true is too nice and tidy but when those desires go haywire, that's a lot more fun."

Claire-Dee Lim originally planned for the webseries adaptation of *The Power Object* to be an animated creation using Flash but discovered that her artistic abilities were not necessarily up to the task. She thus turned to the idea of home-crafted dolls instead, and the concept suits *The Power Object* well. The likes of *Robot Chicken* has made the narrative device a comedic medium in its own right and in the hands of Lim and *The Power Object*, it adds to the overall humor of the webseries—the life-size bottles of wine, martini glasses and other items that are used as props on the show are just as funny as the overall plot. A narrator keeps the action focused and centered, meanwhile, and the storyline itself is both entertaining and engaging to the point that one actually forgets that the world of *The Power Object* is populated by Barbie-like dolls rather than actual human beings.

The one-sentence tagline of *The Power Object* may sound far-fetched but when it comes to execution, the webseries is right on target. Claire-Dee Lim has done an outstanding job of not only writing a comic-filled script that is likewise grounded in reality despite containing a supernatural element, but turning the "watch what you wish for" narrative into a first-class webseries as well. Which just goes to show that one should never judge a book by its cover—especially when that book contains a spell capable of transforming a handcrafted sex device into the source of magical power.

July 4, 2011

Pueblo

Woody Allen is a New Yorker, born and raised. For close to forty years, the acclaimed writer/director used the Big Apple as the setting for his films and incorporated the backdrop of the city in numerous scenes. This is most evident in the 1979 feature *Manhattan*, which was filmed in black-and-white and served as a cinemagraphic homage to the city itself. In 2005, Allen broke with tradition and began using European locales for his movies, including London (*Match Point*), Spain (*Vicky Cristina Barcelona*) and Paris (*Midnight in Paris*). In addition to being critically applauded for their narratives, each of the films also served as little postcards for their respective cities with key architecture and landscapes featured prominently.

While not as ambitious as a Woody Allen film, the webseries *Pueblo* contains many of the same ingredients that have served Allen so successfully through the years. Conceived by two Americans teaching English in the small Spanish town of La Puerta de Segura, the series itself follows an American named Ben (Ben Raznick) as he adapts to life in the same city under the pretext of having arrived in Spain to likewise teach English in the local schools. In reality, however, *Pueblo* is just as much of a "love letter" to the area as *Manhattan* was to New York, while its narrative is a classic Allen-esque tale of love, discover and the search for personal meaning in one's life.

Creators Eve Richer and Ben Raznick utilize the surrounding area of La Puerta de Segura effectively, highlighting many of the elements that define the small Spanish town. Yearly-held festivals and celebrations serve as the backdrop for many of the episodes of *Pueblo*, while the lifestyle of the residents is given proper recognition in brief explorations of the economic fabric of La Puerta de Segura, including the olive and asparagus industries. In fact, each installment of *Pueblo* features a brief "brought to you by" message containing a component of Spanish life. Richer and Raznick even use local townsfolk as actors in the webseries, giving the production a local flavor to go along with the main "fish-out-of-water" narrative centered on American Ben.

While Ben himself may not be modeled on the traditional main protagonist of a Woody Allen film, the character has an innocent charm about him nonetheless and a sly comic wit in terms of observation. "As soon as I got off the bus, it smelled like olive oil," he remarks in the first episode. "I had a meeting with someone at the school at noon to talk about my new job but I guess I missed it. There's nobody at the school right now and it appears to be siesta time." Ben also has a more contemporary version of the flighty Annie Hall in Eva (Eve Richer), a pseudo-girlfriend who has remained in the United States. "I feel like I'm having an existential identity crisis," she tells Ben via web conferencing. "Or I don't even know. I'm kind of torn 'cause I feel like I'm having a post-modern conceptual crisis."

"So you're having a crisis because you don't know which crisis you're having?" a confused Ben replies back, to which Eva

64

responds, "Right, exactly. Thank you. You are the only person that understands me."

Just as the two main female leads of *Vicky Cristina Barcelona* find themselves drawn to an attractive and exotic Spanish male, Ben likewise develops a relationship with a local beauty by the name of Erika Martinez. Their budding and volatile romance serves as the crux of the main narrative within *Pueblo*, but complications arise late in the series as Ben's assignment in La Puerta de Segura winds down and Eva announces that she is coming to Spain for the summer. Like Scarlett Johansson in *Vicky Cristina Barcelona*, Ben realizes in the end that the journey of self-discover is both long and arduous, with brief encounters along the way that turn into mere memories as the road continues.

Of course, in the Wood Allen film, Johansson's Spanish love interest is portrayed by Academy Award-winning actor Javier Bardem. In *Pueblo*, meanwhile, Ben's female counterpart Erika Martinez is a mannequin head. While the use of the inanimate object is never acknowledged within the episodes, the device adds another Allen staple—the offbeat comedy—into the webseries, and in the hands of creators Eve Richer and Ben Raznick, it is effective. "I say, 'Erika, when I go back to the U.S. I'm going to put you in my suitcase," Ben tells the camera in episode four of *Pueblo*. "But that's silly. I'd have to buy her a seat." In a later installment, he discovers a pregnancy test in Erika's purse and confronts her, only to later lament about the difficulty of conversing with the opposite sex as the mannequin head simply stares back in his direction with a blank expression.

65

"Foreigners rarely visit Jaén when they travel to Spain, so we though it would be interesting to document our year there by creating a show about it," Eve Richer explained to AlexandriaNews.org in June 2011 in regards to both the region where La Puerta de Segura is located and the seeds of *Pueblo*. "One of the benefits of living in a small town was that it was easy to get to know people and learn about the culture," Ben Raznick adds. "In the show everyone is very welcoming to my character when he arrives, and luckily that was true for us in real life too."

In the 1985 Woody Allen classic *The Purple Rose of Cairo*, Mia Farrow falls in love with a character—Tom Baxter—from the latest major motion picture playing at the Depression-era theater in her New Jersey hometown. When Baxter literally breaks down the "fourth wall" and walks off the screen and into Farrow's life, the two begin a romance just as unlikely as that between Ben and Erika Martinez from *Pueblo*. "I just met a wonderful new man," Mia Farrow remarks in *The Purple Rose of Cairo*. "He's fictional but you can't have everything."

Fortunately the same does not hold true for *Pueblo*—with its cinemagraphic use of small town Spain, unique wit, overabundance of charm and effective use of the offbeat, this romantic comedy webseries does indeed have everything, and then some.

July 18, 2011

The Real Girl's Guide to Everything Else

The World Wide Web has often been compared to a great equalizer, the bridge that spans the gap created by the simple fact that the majority of media outlets in the United States are controlled by a small handful of conglomerates. Voices and viewpoints seldom heard in the past have now been given a soapbox of their own, for instance, while musically-talented bands who might never have been signed to a major label can find fan-supported success on their own as well. Although this "equalization" has resulted in a lot of mediocre noise, the intelligent and talented have still managed to rise above the clutter and get their opinions and creations across to the masses.

The same promise holds true with the webseries medium. Television creation is an arduous process filled with network interference and creative compromises. Most of all, television is a business which traditionally has attracted the "safe" and "popular" instead of taking risks on less mainstream projects. While the television medium has had its share of quality shows and remains the premier storytelling device of our times, many non-traditional narratives have no doubt been left on the wayside. Yet again, however, where corporate media fails the Internet has stepped in. A prime example is *The Real Girl's Guide to Everything Else*, a comedic webseries focusing on a feminist lesbian journalist and her attempt to write a book about Afghanistani women.

When her agent nixes the idea and threatens to terminate their professional relationship, Rasha (Robin Dalea) is convinced by her friends Vanna (Nikki Brown), Sydney (Reene Dutt) and Angie (Carmen Elena Mitchell) to write a chick-lit novel—"those books with the pink covers and the bubbly-font chapter headings where the main character's always looking for Mister Right and maxing out her credit cards along the way"—as a means to raise the necessary funds to travel to Afghanistan. But while her friends are straight and fashionably progressive, Rasha has never been with a man and prefers combat boots to Jimmy Choos. Her friends thus decide to educate her on the traditional female lifestyle as a form of research, hooking her up with a pair of booty shorts and a True-Love-Always-Forever-dot-com dating profile.

In many ways *The Real Girl's Guide to Everything Else* resembles an anti-*Sex and the City*, an intentional comparison made obvious at the start of each episode as the webseries mimics the HBO show's iconic opening credits sequence. The four main characters also share their thoughts over lunch and a large amount of the dialogue centers on humorous-but-frank sexual discussions. Rasha, for instance, explains to her male pseudo-date that not all women wax their private parts. "You know that women's pubic hair doesn't grow in neat, skinny, little rectangular landing strips naturally, right?" she asks when he seems confused.

This is not to suggest that the webseries is a parody or *Sex and the City* wannabe—*The Real Girl's Guide to Everything Else* is quality entertainment in its own right and any references to its HBO counterpart only adds to the enjoyment. The first three episodes are the most entertaining as Rasha navigates her way through high heels and superficial guys, all the while attempting to keep her life-partner Liz (Jennifer Weaver) reassured that she is not changing into someone else just weeks before their wedding. Their pillow-talk conversation about Rasha's recently-waxed vagina coupled with Liz's Naomi Wolf-style feminist ranting, for instance, is a classic. The second half of the six-episode first season maintains the humor and insightful observations but seems a little rushed from a narrative standpoint. Still, the webseries concludes in a fulfilling manner and a sense of resolution that also leaves the door open for more installments.

"The idea came out my growing frustration with a lot of mainstream television shows and films marketed towards women," creator Carmen Elena Mitchell explained to CherryGrrl.com in March 2010. "I felt like I wasn't seeing myself in these movies. I wasn't seeing my friends. I wasn't hearing our conversations. Why was everything about chasing unavailable men and pining over expensive footwear? Where were the conversations about politics, books, art, and our careers? And while I'm not anti-fashion, anti-relationship, or anti-girly-girl, I feel like there's so much more to explore in women's lives."

With only a handful of companies owning the vast majority of television networks and cable channels in the country, as well as the difficulty of breaking into the industry and finding success, it is doubtful that Carmen Elena Mitchell would have had the opportunity to tell her version of life and friendship through mainstream media. By combining quality writing and acting, along with top-notch directing by Heather de Michele, Mitchell instead created a solid and funny webseries that not only adds to the entertainment value of the budding new genre, but proves that the Internet can be the defining equalizer for television just as it has been for other mediums.

March 28, 2010

Saving Rent

Taking a diverse assortment of characters that would not normally interact and placing them together in an offbeat environment is a time-honored comic tradition. Slews of serial narratives, from *Gilligan's Island* to *The Office* on television as well as such webseries as *The Guild* and *The Video Makers* online, have utilized the plot device both effectively and successfully. *Saving Rent* follows in similar footsteps with a twelve-episode season that is both funny and relevant while again proving that an independently-produced webseries can be just as enjoyable as any sitcom on television.

Advertising manager Mike (Vincent Giovanni) and girlfriend Kelley (Alice Cutler) relocate from Boston to Los Angeles only to find life on the West Coast different than expected when Mike loses his job due to a weakened economy. With his life-savings spent on a luxurious home and his pride preventing him from telling Kelley that about his unemployment status, Mike hatches a plan to rent out the extra rooms in their large abode to a small handful of strangers. After interviewing the usual assortment of suspects—or in this case, unusual assortment—the two decide upon Paul (Jacob Lane), a Canadian trying to make it as an actor in L.A.; Suzie (Mallory McGill), a waitress who insists she is twenty-one despite looking much younger; Tina (Ashley Palmer), a wannabe porn-star; and Chucho (Alex Ruiz), a seemingly illegal Mexican immigrant who doesn't speak English.

Having thus set up the situation in the first episode, co-creators Gary Teperman and Ernie Lee then develop the comedy by exploring this oddball collection of roommates and the lengths they go to in order to achieve personal success. With a premise already built on one lie—the fact that Mike lost his job but still pretends to go to work everyday—*Saving Rent* expands upon it by giving each member of the ensemble cast secrets and lies of their own.

While Paul is not above dropping the name William Shatner as a reference during his initial rental interview with Mike and Kelley, for instance, he is in actuality the epitome of a struggling actor in Los Angeles and is forced to take such meandering jobs as portraying a pirate on Hollywood Boulevard and a fake patient for medical students to diagnose. Suzie, meanwhile, is not a twenty-one-year-old world traveler but a teenage runaway, and while Tina does have the ambition to be an adult film start, she has yet to break into the industry. It also turns out that Chucho is neither Mexican nor unable to speak English, and even Kelley gets into the act by secretly selling weed and marijuana-laced brownies on the side.

Each episode of the webseries begins with a short, thirty-second opening sequence featuring a theme-song reminiscent of any number of television sitcoms produced by Norman Lear in the 1970s and 80s. While *Saving Rent* may not be a classic along the likes of *All in the Family*, *Maude* and *The Jeffersons*, it is just as much an exploration of its times as those legendary Lear shows of the past. In the 1970s, it was racial and gender inequality that were the country's primary struggles; for the years 2008-2010, it's the economy and the struggles of every day Americans who have faced lay-offs and difficulty making ends meet. While Mike may be more middle-to-upper class economically as opposed to working class, the situation of suddenly finding himself unemployed and potentially losing his home because of an inability to pay his mortgage is just as much a sign of the times as anything else.

Of course, the growing webseries medium itself is another staple of the times in which we live, something not lost on the cast and crew of *Saving Rent*. "We always intended to shoot it as a webseries," Alice Cutler, who not only portrays wife Kelley but served as an executive producer and writer on the show, told *Somojo Magazine* in October 2009. "More and more people are watching TV on the Internet, higher profile actors are appearing on webseries, and it's so easy to promote online content. And with sites like Facebook and Twitter, you can get the word out to thousands instantly without spending a dime."

With its classic premise and relevant subject matter, *Saving Rent* is a situation comedy for our uncertain economic times that fits in nicely with other webseries of its genre. It is also a show that anyone can identify with—who hasn't, after all, lied to both others and themselves about the various crossroads that life sometimes leads. *Saving Rent* proves that we are not alone with

73

the struggles we face, and helps us to both gain perspective and laugh along the way as well. What could be more right for the times than that?

April 5, 2010

SOLO

Shortly after the turn of the century, network television saw an influx of reality show programming. While many proved to have both an entertaining and quality value associated with them, a large portion were derivative and inane. For every *Survivor*, for instance, there was a *Temptation Island*. For every *Amazing Race*, there was *The Swan*. And for every *American Idol*, there was *I Know My Kid's a Star*. Suffice it to say, if ever there was a genre that just screamed to be spoofed, it was reality television.

The webseries medium has already witnessed one satirical take, *The Video Makers*, which featured a behind-the-scenes look at an independent production company manufacturing such fare as *Pets of the Third Reich* and *Chefs Behind Bars*. There is obviously enough room on the World Wide Web for additional comedic spoofs of reality television, however, as the very funny and highly original *SOLO* has proven. After successfully producing a string of successful series like *Divorce Swapping* and *Big Brother's My Lover*, fictitious mogul Jack Spratt (Jay Caputo) has taken the genre to the next level by blasting an individual into space and creating a reality show around his one-man mission to Mars. Only one problem—after a mere thirty days, the show is cancelled and Spratt's funds have dried up.

Created by Jonathan Nail, *SOLO* thus not only features the misadventures of Scott Drizhal (portrayed by Nail) as he finds himself trapped on a spaceship with only an artificial intelligence computer named PHAL (voiced by Jason Burns)—in homage to the notorious HAL from *2001: A Space Odyssey*—but those of Spratt, the two remaining "mission control" employees he is still able to afford and Drizhal's attractive and angry wife, Rebecca (Michele Boyd).

Nail, who has appeared on such television shows as *Mad Men* and *Criminal Minds*, had been kicking around the idea of creating his own series or film for some time before realizing the growing potential of the new online video medium. Once he decided to produce a webseries instead, it was just a matter of finding the right narrative. "It had to fit in with what I could afford, it had to fit in with a story I was interested in," he told *Clicker* in July 2010. "I've always been interested in sci-fi and fantasy. I'm a huge fan of *Hitchhiker's Guide to the Galaxy*. Douglas Adams is a huge inspiration of me. At the end of the day, it's a character study that was formulating in my brain early in 2009, so I started putting the pieces together."

The character elements of *SOLO* are evident within the first three episodes of the series. Drizhal experiences a full range of emotions upon learning that his mission has been cancelled mid-flight, progressing from the original fear and anxiety of being trapped alone in space, with possibly no way of returning home, all the way through the five stages of grief—denial, anger, bargaining, depression and acceptance. In one of the many laugh-out-loud scenes from *SOLO*, Drizhal even reaches out to President Barack Obama for assistance. "Fire up the space shuttle and rescue me," he pleads. "I'll do anything you want, you can double my taxes." In the end, the leader of the free world not only doesn't know who Drizhal is, but concludes that it's merely a prank. "Did Palin put you up to this?" he asks.

But *SOLO* is not simply about Drizhal and his attempts to cope with the suddenly dire situation he finds himself in. A spaceflight of any kind requires a large team of scientists, engineers and an assortment of other experts in order for it to succeed. Because of the reality show's cancellation, however, and the subsequent lack of funds, "mission control" is quickly reduced to a two-person staff consisting of Ratish Gupta (Amol Shah) and Gerry Simon (Melissa Dalton) and relocated to Drizhal's suburban home. Producer Jack Spratt has also apparently borrowed money from the Japanese mafia, which in turn wants immediate payback. Add Rebecca Drizhal—who discovers that her husband has been unemployed for nine months and is thus out of money as well—and one has all the ingredients for a classic screwball comedy.

When it came time to produce *SOLO*, Jonathan Nail abandoned the prospect of filming on the cheap and utilized his initial resources to create three quality episodes instead. Taking a cue from Felicia Day and *The Guild*, he also set up a means for fans to donate in order to assist with future installments. Nail reasoned that by first creating buzz—as well as demonstrating the capabilities and potential of *SOLO*—it would then be easier to acquire the necessary funding to complete an ambitious three seasons and twenty-seven episodes for his creation.

"We are currently looking for more sponsorship, but the hard part right now is proving return on investment," Nail explained to *Clicker*. "Our show is created in a way that it is a welcome opportunity for sponsors to jump in at this moment. Now that we've created these three episodes, anyone could become a sponsor of the show with very little money and get a lot of coverage."

Based on the first three episodes, Jonathan Nail has indeed created not only a professionally produced webseries but an original and entertaining one at that. And by not simply jumping into the medium fray but studying both the pros and cons of the fledgling online video industry first, he has also positioned *SOLO* to not only become a successful webseries in its on right but a potential benchmark for other creators to aspire and a business model to emulate.

Not bad for a show that was "cancelled."

July 26, 2010

Time for Passion

Within the realms of both theater and screen, there are many approaches to the vocation of acting. The famed American teacher Lee Strasberg, for instance, introduced the term "method acting" into the vernacular when he advocated that his students utilize their own emotions and memories within their performances. Strasberg in turn was heavily influenced by the works of Constantin Stanislavski, who perfected a holistic approach in which the actor experienced the role both inside and outside of themselves. Even Sir Laurence Olivier was not above giving advice to his colleagues in regards to technique, most notably to Dustin Hoffman while filming *Marathon Man*. When Hoffman appeared on set after having stayed awake for twenty-four straight hours because his character had done so as well, Olivier remarked, "My dear boy, why don't you try acting?"

Then there's Johnson Roberts of the webseries *Time for Passion*. "I developed these tips from lifetime achievement of auditioning over fifty times," he remarks during a short video advertisement for his acting school. "Together, tips spell out 'JOHNSON.'" Roberts then introduces nineteen brief guidelines for struggling actors that inevitably have nothing to do with the letters in his first name. "If you are not so good at acting, wear sunglasses to your addition," he explains in broken English while on the letter J. Under H, meanwhile, Johnson Roberts suggests, "Always pause before you say your line. It shows that you were thinking and you didn't just memorize your scene."

The webseries proper is filmed documentary-style and intersperses scenes from Roberts' acting class with the main character's attempts at filming his own original script, entitled *The World*. "It will deal with love, sex, drugs, betrayal, et cetera," he explains. "It is like one of those bagels with egg, poppy seed, onion, garlic, cheese." The manuscript contains scratch-and-sniff decals to add to the authenticity of the narrative, offering smells of basements and landfills to go along with the dialogue. As Johnson Roberts explains to his would-be director, he has named the concept "Scratch 'N Script."

Although Roberts declares that he has read over forty scripts throughout his lifetime and thus feels knowledgeable enough to write his own film, his major problem with producing it is finding the necessary actors capable of portraying the characters within. As opposed to the Strasberg or Stanislavski methods—or even that of Laurence Olivier—Johnson Roberts believes that passion is the key to great acting.

"So many times I see movies where there is no passion," he tells his class. "Like Don Corleone in *The Godfather*. When Marlon Brando hears that his only son of three sons, Sonny Corleone, is dead, what does he do? Nothing! Quiet, silence." The teacher then demonstrates what he would do as he proceeds to emotionally erupt over the news of Sonny's death. "Then I would break a lamp, picture frame or kick in a window," he concludes. "That is passion."

In addition to episodes of the actual webseries, the *Time for Passion* website—or "websight," as Johnson Roberts calls it—is filled with information about the both the man and his acting class. There are also other videos that are not part of the main narrative but compliment the *Time for Passion* experience nonetheless. In addition to the previously mentioned introductory advertisement in which Johnson Roberts offers acting tips, for instance, there is a review of the movie *Rayne Man*. Not only does Roberts skewer the title of the 1988 film, but he refers to the two stars of the comedy-drama as Dustin Hoffa and Jerry Maguire and details an *X-Men* style plot in which the title character can control the weather.

The Johnson Roberts ego is likewise on full display. The "about" page of the website asks such rhetorical questions as "Who do you think started Billy Joel's fire?" and "Who do you think tell Freddy Mercury to start village people?" The running gag not only continues in video form during the webseries—"Who do you think told Oscar Mayer to start giving out acting awards?"—but carries over onto the *Time for Passion* Facebook page ("Who do you think taught Smokey Robison that only he can prevent forest fires?") and Twitter posts ("Who do you think convinced country to name itself after cuba gooding junior?").

Time for Passion writer/director Kor Adana and Amol Shah, the New Jersey-born actor who portrays Johnson Roberts, have thus not only created a likeable character but taken advantage of the Internet and social media to further advance the enjoyment of the webseries proper and keep viewers entertained beyond merely watching the episodes. Shah has appeared on such television shows as *Grey's Anatomy* and *Brothers & Sisters*, and likewise had a role in the reality-spoof webseries *Solo*. His portrayal of Johnson Roberts, meanwhile, exudes the necessary amount of egotistical confidence, misguided innocence and natural charm to raise the character beyond that of mere buffoon or blowhard and into a memorable comedic classic in his own right.

But don't take my word for it, just ask Johnson Roberts—I'm sure he would agree. After all, "Who do you think told Steven Spielberg to make T-Rex bigger than all other dinosaurs in *Jurassic Park*?"

May 16, 2011

Vampire Mob

Vampires have become a hot commodity as of late. From the *Twilight* move franchise to the Emmy-nominated HBO drama *True Blood*, it seems that America has a huge appetite for the blood-sucking fiends. But the country also has a fascination with the criminal mobster, a love-hate relationship that goes back decades to the original *The Godfather* and extends all the way to another Emmy-honored HBO series, *The Sopranos*. Now Boston bred Joe Wilson has found a way to combine these two genres into the humanly realistic, often humorous and entirely gripping webseries, *Vampire Mob*.

Don Grigioni, the main antagonist of the series, may be a member of the undead but he is no Edward from *Twilight* or Bill from *True Blood*. There is no moping in *Vampire Mob*, no tormented souls or seeking of redemption either. In fact, Don and his wife Annie are practically human in every way possible except that they drink blood for nutrition and cannot go outside during the daytime. "I wouldn't choose it but it's pretty good," Annie tells her sister in regards to being a vampire. "I mean, I've lost weight. I feel great. I was always trying to stay out of the sun anyways. And Don and I... I think it brought us closer. I mean, we're the only ones who understand each other, what it's like."

Although Don is a member of the mob in addition to being a vampire, he is also not Michael Corleone or Tony Soprano. Instead of being a crime boss, he's a mere hit man who drains the blood from his victims and brings it home in large jugs to share with his wife. "Gotta love mixing business with grocery shopping," Don remarks. When the pickings prove slim, he muses about having to take on more jobs and even purchases a synthetic brand, similar to *True Blood*, from Marty Five's Castle and New Organic Dispensary.

Vampire Mob is filmed as a documentary/reality show with Don's unseen nephew Mikey working the camera. In addition to showcasing the action of the webseries, the narrative device offers the opportunity for the characters to privately share their thoughts with the audience, much like the NBC comedy *The Office*. "I was shot," Don tells the camera in the first episode. "And then I did the whole 'light at the end of the tunnel' thing. Heard voices. Annoying voices. Relatives' voices. Voices of... business associates? So I chose this. You know, live forever hopefully. Most of my business is done at night—it's a good fit."

His initial reaction to the transformation was positive, especially in regards to his wife. "I though it would be good for our marriage," Don explains. "I could relax because there'd be more wives. *They* wouldn't live forever." But although he tells Annie that the reason he eventually turned her into a vampire was because he loved her, in reality Don's action stemmed from the simple fact that he was hungry. Annie, however, has no such hidden motives when it comes to her own family. "If I'm going to live forever, I want my mother to live forever," she remarks to the camera. "So I can complain about Don."

"Now I've got a wife and a mother-in-law that are going to live with me for eternity," Don Grigioni in turn confides, his voice dripping with both regret and fear. Therein lies the true brilliance of *Vampire Mob*—while the webseries may indeed be a masterful mash-up of the vampire and mobster genres, in reality it's the spot-on story of a dysfunctional middle class family struggling to get along with each other.

"I was working as a bartender in Cambridge about a decade ago and the local Mafia Don would come in on a daily basis," creator Joe Wilson told the *Indianapolis Examiner* in June 2010 regarding the background of the webseries. "He'd grease all the employees with his daily strategy. He'd tell the manager, 'If my wife calls, tell her I left at one,' then he'd leave and it would be eleven p.m. He'd repeat the same story to all the staff that he knew and he'd do it everyday. His wife would call and everybody'd stick to the story. All the men in the bar knew him and feared him, but we'd make mention of his wife and he'd turn white and look around like the FBI was barging in."

In addition to the exploration of family within *Vampire Mob*, the webseries humanizes its characters in other ways as well. "I miss meatballs," Don tells the camera about his inability to now eat like a regular person. "Huge meatballs with gravy. I could care less about the pasta." And despite the fact that food consumption gives them "the runs for a couple of days," he still makes Annie cook dinner. "I like to sit down and feel like I'm having a meal," he explains before feeding his plate to the dog.

While the initial advent of the webseries as a creative medium resulted in a rush of productions that were poorly filmed and written, *Vampire Mob* joins a number of recent projects that benefit from strong writing and directing. Joe Wilson produced *Vampire Mob* as part of the new Screen Actors Guild guidelines regarding webseries, which gave him access to professional performers like John Colella (Don Grigioni), Reamy Hall (Annie) and Chris Mulkey, adding to the quality of the finished project.

"Don't get me wrong, I would love to be working with a big studio or have the ability to finance something on a larger scale," Wilson told the *Examiner* in regards to *Vampire Mob*. "But what we're doing is just fine, and it allows incredible freedom at a very low cost."

Joe Wilson has created a webseries that is as much a combination of offbeat humor and dysfunctional family drama as it is a mix of the vampire and mobster genres that, amazingly enough, works on all of those levels. While *Vampire Mob* may never achieve Emmy recognition on par with *The Sopranos* or *True Blood*, it is a creative equal to those series nonetheless and gives new meaning to the phrase, "Take a bite out of crime."

September 22, 2010

The Variants

It has become cool to be a geek. One of the most successful television sitcoms in recent years, for instance, is the CBS series *The Big Bang Theory*, which features two genius male protagonists who spend their free time playing video games and collecting comic books. Then there's the webseries *The Guild*, about a group of *World of Warcraft* type gamers that has built a significant online fanbase for itself. Adding to this growing list of geek-centric entertainment is another webseries, *The Variants*, which follows the ongoing antics at real-world Dallas comic book store, Zeus Comics.

"Crazy stuff happens at the comic shop," Zeus owner Richard Neal explains of the show's inception. "Something about the mix of nerds and retail leads to some absurd situations that just get funnier when you retell them. I thought there was something there, so I called my friends to help document it."

Neal's original plan was to film a straight-forward reality series, but after meeting with Joe Cucinotti and Ken Lowry—two local actors/writers in the Dallas area who were also regular customers at Zeus—a fictionalized version was created instead. Well, kind of. "Our set is the actual store," Cucinotti explains. "Other than Ken and myself, our main cast consists of people who really work behind the counter. Many of the extras and minor characters are played by loyal customers of the store. While we exaggerate some of the events, the presentation is still very authentic."

Each episode of *The Variants* is crafted as a stand-alone installment and centers upon specific comic book store events, such as the release of a rare variant edition or guest signers to boost sales, as well as general retail situations like offbeat and crazed customers. While comparisons to filmmaker Kevin Smith may immediately come to mind—Cucinotti's character even dresses up as Silent Bob at one point—this webseries is more of a homage to the comic book community at large than simply another transplanted update of *Clerks*.

Similarities also exist between *The Variants* and both *The Big Bang Theory* and *The Guild*, all of which feature crisp dialogue and snappy one-liners that can be enjoyed by both geeks and non-geeks alike. In the episode "Passholes," for instance, a group of zombie-esque customers trap the characters in the comic book store after closing. When Richard (Neal) suggests they should go to the mall to escape the mob, Joe (Cucinotti) replies, "Dude, have you even seen a zombie movie?" Other classic lines include, "It sounds like all those fanboys when they found out Disney bought Marvel" and, "Season eight? There was something after season five?"—a reference to the latest *Buffy the Vampire Slayer* comic.

The fifth installment of the webseries, entitled "Guest Signing," is a true comedy classic that best illustrates the show's ability to wrap its comic book references with mass-appealing humor. In the episode, real-life illustrator Dave Crosland and webcomic creator Scott Kurtz make an appearance at Zeus Comics and portray fictionalized versions of themselves: Crosland is clueless with a Zen-like simplicity while Kurtz is simply an obnoxious blowhard. The comedy thus lies in the exaggerated nature of these actual artists, which in turn makes the various situations the staff at Zeus Comics find themselves in humorous regardless if one knows who Dave Crosland and Scott Kurtz are or not.

Although each episode contains a standalone narrative, *The Variants* also features season-long threads involving the financial viability of the store and Joe's apparent crush on fellow co-worker Keli (Keli Wolf). References to past storylines are also sprinkled throughout, including Joe's fondness for Kurt Russell movies and an older gentlemen intent on selling his dead friend's comic book collection in order to pay for the funeral. In addition to store owner Richard, the loveable goof-off Joe and level-headed Keli, the main cast is rounded out with crusty sales clerk Barry (Barry Furhman) and stockroom guy Vlad (Lowery), who hides in the back when not attempting to cloak himself in a field of invisibility.

In real life, Zeus Comics is a prestigious establishment that not only has received numerous awards in the Dallas area, including "Best of Big D" from *D Magazine*, but was also honored with the 2006 Will Eisner Spirit of Retailer Excellence Award. In *The Variants*, meanwhile, the fictitious Zeus Comics is home to an entertaining cast of characters that generates plenty of laugh-at-loud moments for both the geek-initiated and society-at-large.

Either institution is also the type of store that Leonard Hofstadter and Sheldon Cooper of the CBS sitcom *The Big Bang Theory* would feel comfortable entering in order to purchase the latest comic book adaptation of the online webseries *The Guild*.

June 14, 2010

The Video Makers

Walter Gottlieb has an impressive resume as an independent video producer. A 1983 graduate from NYU Film School, he eventually started his own company, Final Cut Productions, in the Washington DC area in the mid-90s. Since then, Gottlieb and Final Cut have produced numerous non-fiction programs for such luminaries as PBS, the Smithsonian and National Geographic, and was even nominated for two Emmy awards for its "Silver Springs: Story of an American Suburb" special in 2002.

So when Gottlieb decided to write and produce his first webseries, spoofing the industry that he has been both "part of" and "successful in" over the years seemed the logical place to start. *The Video Makers* accomplishes that and much more—its satirical take on not just documentary television but "reality" shows as well is a very funny critique about how far the genre has digressed in recent times, while its ensemble cast of offbeat characters is on par with many classic comedies of the past.

Former college sweethearts Kevin Sellers (Lee Ordeman) and Amanda Stuart (Ann Marie Barbour) are the co-founders of Lowball Production, a video company which produces both documentaries and reality shows for cable networks like the Exculpatory Channel, Esophagus Network and Hysteria Channel. Only in business for a mere six months, they are already

91

struggling to keep their company afloat as production snafus and budget overruns are beginning to take their toll.

Doug Van Houten (Charlie Davidson), meanwhile, is the staff videographer who is having an affair with junior producer Spark Bishop (Mundy Spears). Joel Hummberger (Jake Koenig), another junior producer, is finding the transition from his previous job— where he worked on documentaries for PBS—to his current one at Lowball difficult at best. Then there's Shawn Coolidge (Brandon Dorsey), who used to edit music videos in New York before making the move to non-fiction television.

While seemingly normal on the outside, this collection of characters is anything but. The majority of Doug and Spark's sexual encounters, for instance, tend to occur in the most unusual of environments, from inside a coffin to locked in an actual jail cell. Despite having graduated college years ago, as well as the fact that Amanda is now married with children, Kevin still believes there is a sexual attraction between the two of them. Kevin is also on two forms of medication—anti-depressants and sleeping pills—which causes problems when he takes the wrong one at the wrong time. Then there's the amusing aspect of seeing Joel, who is Jewish, working on the documentary, *Pets of the Third Reich*.

While the employees of Lowball Productions are entertaining enough, it is the television reality shows and documentaries they are producing that elevates *The Video Makers* into a truly funny spoof on both the business and society in general. While in past years network television has had its share of ludicrous reality concepts—including *The Littlest Groom*, *Amish in the City* and *Temptation Island*—Lowball takes the concept to even more ridiculous levels. In addition to *Pets of the Third Reich* ("the fuehrer was especially fond of hamsters"), there is *Chefs Behind Bars* and a prison makeover show.

One highlight is *Top Shots*, a competition show where bikini-clad women shoot each other with Airsoft rifles in order to be named the best markswomen in America. The elimination sequence features the participant who has fallen victim to the most "hits" being handed a bouquet of funeral flowers and then escorted into a casket. The losers do not go quietly, however—one eliminated girl vows, "I'm going to come back in the afterlife and I'm going to haunt your asses." Another contestant uses an actual taser and declares afterwards, "That's for wearing my bikini bottoms, bitch."

To supplement their income, Lowball Productions also creates corporate videos for outside clients. But even here the subject matter tends to veer towards the absurd—one client wants to open a customer service call-center in the United States that assists users in India. "The Indian middle-class is growing, the American middle-class is shrinking," he explains. "We've got folks here desperate for work, and upperly-mobile people in India who need customer service." Lowball Productions is brought in to produce the training video, which includes a segment on the need for all of the workers to be fluent in Hindi.

The Video Makers is both a fun and funny take on the non-fiction television business, a behind the scenes spoof of the industry and a clever statement in regards to the current state of pop culture in general. Walter Gottlieb has proven that not only is he able to create genuine documentaries for the worlds of PBS and National Geographic, but has a solid sense of humor in regards to the medium as well.

March 1, 2010

We Are with the Band

Bands have always attracted groupies. In the late 1960s, for instance, a group of hardcore Beatles fans used to hang around both the Apple Corp building and Abbey Road Studios in London. Known as "Apple Scruffs," they were immortalized in both the George Harrison song of the same name as well as Paul McCartney's "She Came in Through the Bathroom Window," a reference to when some of them broke into his home via, appropriately enough, an upstairs window. Then there was Pamela Des Barres, who became a regular feature in the Los Angeles music scene during the same time period and eventually had sexual trysts with everyone from Jim Morrison to Mick Jagger to Jimmy Page.

The webseries *We Are with the Band* focuses on a pair of modern day groupies, Elle Franklin (Heleya de Barros) and Marci Kline (Vivian Kerr), as they attempt to party their way through life while inevitably "living the dream." During the course of the episodes, the two Los Angeles hipsters experience more misadventure than adventure when their names are not included on a nightclub's VIP list, attempt to cleanse their bodies with a mixed concoction of lemon juice, maple syrup and cayenne, and fail to attend a warehouse party because they passed out on their front lawn after overindulging on vodka.

In many ways, Elle and Marci are more wannabes than actual groupies and have an air of naïve innocence about them as they fashion their cutting edge lifestyle. The so-called "dream" that they are living includes a fair amount of independence, the lack of traditional employment and plenty of alcohol. There is a genuine chemistry between the two leads and the dynamics of the pair, with Elle as the leader and Marci as the follower, is played with a loveable charm that adds to the authentic feel of the series.

The eight episodes that make up the first season are short, lasting anywhere from three to five minutes each, but writer Vivian Kerr is able to pack enough "story" into that time span to make them entertaining nonetheless. Comparisons to another Los Angeles-based webseries that follows the lives of its female characters, *Fourplay in LA*, quickly come to mind—that series likewise has shorter episodes, but while they are more standalone narratives, *We Are with the Band* has a serial quality that is best viewed when all of the installments are watched concurrently.

We Are with the Band also shares the same level of quality dialogue as *Fourplay in LA* and is filled with a plethora of catchy one-liners. Examples include: "He's corporate, he takes yoga and has health insurance;" "This is going to be an important night for us, Marci—I feel like Obama on election night;" "Why does our social life have to be dictated by these velvet rope whores?;" "Fashion is a big part of fitness;" "(Liver damage) only happens after thirty;" "Every time they change their name it's like a new band;" and "What are we waiting for? We only have four hours to get ready and new fishnets do not buy themselves."

While television is often a male-dominated industry, it is refreshing to see a new wave of female writers making their debut via the webseries medium. The list not only includes Kerr of *We Are with the Band* and Hillary Rhodes from *Fourplay in LA*, but Carmen Elena Mitchell of *The Real Girl's Guide to Everything Else* as well. The fact that their talents have been realized outside of traditional Hollywood is a testament to the equalizing promise of the Internet, and for the creators of *We Are with the Band*, that may have even been the point.

Heleya de Barros and Vivian Kerr met at the University of Southern California and eventually found there way to Los Angeles. Actors by trade, they formed a production company in 2009, DK Productions, that is described on their website as "dedicated to producing ambitious female-driven projects" and "has an ongoing commitment to the development of new work and aims to expand opportunities for women in comedy." *We Are with the Band* is their first endeavor together, and certainly lives up to the mission statement of the partnership.

"We wanted to do a show that was a little bit outside of the mainstream, inspired more by British comedy," Kerr explained to PopCultureMonster.com in May 2010. "There's a lack of humility and self-awareness in Los Angeles which is very funny to me, and hipsters are pretty ripe for parody."

"When we graduated from college Vivian and I started going to see a lot of local music in LA," de Barros further expanded. "As we started to learn the club scene we were blown away by some of the characters we met. Often the 'people watching' between sets was more interesting than the music. When we started to brainstorm about writing a series we thought the hipster scene would make great material. We also thought the idea of these two girls who are trying to find themselves spoke to a large audience. There are a lot of LA specific jokes, but I think anybody can relate to the struggles Elle and Marci deal with."

We Are with the Band certainly fits the criteria set forth by the show's creators and is a humorous portrayal of two young female hipsters exploring the underground band scene in Los Angeles. Elle and Marci may be living a life of misadventure, but with strong acting, memorable dialogue and overall quality, the webseries itself is an enjoyable—and yes, relatable—adventure for viewers everywhere.

August 20, 2010

ABOUT ALTERNA-TV.COM

alterna-tv.com is an online source for news on the changes within the television industry, unique discussions on quality programming and reviews of the webseries medium. Started by Pittsburgh writer Anthony Letizia in 2007, the website has developed a reputation for its in-depth analysis and knowledgeable opinions despite having a smaller, more independent spirit.